Communism and Christ

COMMUNISM
AND
CHRIST

By

CHARLES W. LOWRY

Foreword by
HORACE W. B. DONEGAN
Bishop of New York

MOREHOUSE-GORHAM CO.
New York
1952

PRINTED IN THE UNITED STATES OF AMERICA

BY THE HADDON CRAFTSMEN, INC., SCRANTON, PA.

To My Daughter

HARRIET RICHARDS LOWRY

For eighteen and a half years
a joy without alloy and without decrease

Foreword

BY THE BISHOP OF NEW YORK

ONE OF THE puzzling questions of our time is what books to read among the multitude of printed words which come to our attention every year. It seems appropriate therefore, and indeed a part of my responsibility as Bishop of New York, not only to offer suggestions for reading, but more definitely to sponsor a book for our people. This book is the first of what I trust will be an annual series of "Bishop of New York Books."

The pulpit of the Cathedral of St. John the Divine, in New York, is a natural platform for the presentation of the Christian faith as it applies to some of the bewildering major issues of our age. Part of the content of this present volume was the subject matter of a series of sermons delivered in the Cathedral during the summer of 1951, with large numbers of university students in attendance. Here you will find a brilliant analysis and discussion of the most timely contemporary question—Communism.

Communism does not lend itself to any simple primer type of consideration. It is too complex for that. Perhaps that is the reason why we are content to attack it with slogans. But the employment of prejudices only against such an enemy is certainly not in the best tradition of the Christian faith nor is it effective.

We must seek to understand the origin, history, development and appeal of Communism. It is not enough to condemn what goes on behind the Iron Curtain; we must try to evaluate what goes on there. We shall not conquer it by slogans or propaganda or atomic weapons. Rather in the Christian faith are to be found the undefeatable ideas which are more than a match for the ideology of Communism. But here again it is not enough to be vague and nebulous about what we believe. We must understand more clearly the vast meaning and resources of our faith as followers of Christ.

Communism, as Dr. Lowry points out, is not simply a political system. It is a world religion, bidding for the loyalty of every man, woman, and child. "Religion in its broad sense offers man personal well-being through union with forces and powers greater than himself." In the Asiatic world, where man has been obviously deprived of personal well-being, Communism knocks at the door as a friend of the common man and appears in the disguise of a saviour offering a scheme of salvation, not of the soul, but of the body. Thus a doctrine of man is offered which is superficially attractive, but profoundly inferior to the doctrine of man as a child of God and an inheritor of the Kingdom of God, found in the Christian faith. There is an interesting, tabular comparison of the systems of Christianity and Communism (page 37) which clarifies the distinctions between these two world religions—one bent upon revolution through violence, and the other seeking to change the world through the power of love.

"The Cross means that love is the final truth." This book helps us to evaluate Communism in that light.

Horace W. B. Donegan
Bishop of New York

Preface

THE SUBJECT of the work which follows is Communism and its principal rival for the spiritual allegiance of mankind. The present age, marked by the occurrence of "World" wars and the rise of new totalitarian systems, comes in for considerable attention. The distinctive feature of the book is its treatment of Communism as a new universal salvation religion. Because not a few modern people understand the term "religion" in a qualitative sense, as though its use implied a compliment, I want to make it clear that in treating Communism as a religion, I use the word in the same sense as if I spoke of "the five great living religions" or if I referred to "the religion of the American Indian." The word denotes a certain nature, structure, and functioning, not a judgment of value or usefulness. Like other great and elemental aspects of human feeling and behavior, religion may be very good and it may be very bad.

The background of *Communism and Christ* is a long and intense preoccupation with the ideological and political currents of our day. I was in Germany just prior to Hitler's coming to power and throughout the following decade followed with the utmost interest the course of National Socialism and of Communism and Fascism as well. I may lay claim to being one of the few people whose point of view on the relation between the two really powerful totalitarian systems, National Socialism and Communism, underwent no change. From my first reading of *Mein Kampf*, it was clear that the German article was a kind of *ersatz* Communism, cleverly worked up for home consumption. I was in Europe at the time of the signing of the Russo-

German Pact which touched off World War II. I interpreted it then and have ever since as an agreement between two utterly conscienceless thieves. On the side of Stalin, it was a deliberate design for getting his chief neighbors and adversaries at each other's throats, with the virtual certainty, so he felt, that the result would be a Europe ripe for revolution on the Leninist pattern. The miscalculation of the Russian leader was very nearly total and all but cost him Russia and the whole Communist experiment. Then by one of the really immense ironies of history his allies, Great Britain and the United States, freely arranged things in Europe and in Asia as well so as to give Russian revolutionary imperialism virtually the set-up it had expected to achieve as a result of the war unloosed in 1939. The Russian leaders, who are uninterested in fair play and who are always actuated exclusively by cold-blooded considerations, moved in on all possible fronts, to the surprise and dismay of the pro-Russian policymakers in the Allied Capitals, Washington and London.

What has happened since is familiar to all and has changed the lives of all. The past is past, and is forever unalterable. Sometimes, however, the lamp of experience sheds light on the present journey. Looking back, we can see that the leftist orientation of American and British policy was in part accident, in part the natural bent of American liberalism, and in part the reflex of our inflexibly severe and sadly misguided German policy. The symbol of this was "unconditional surrender." I opposed this from the start on three grounds: (a) that it was Pharisaic and unchristian; (b) that it was uninformed as regarded the complexity of the German situation and mentality under Hitler; and (c) that it revealed abysmal ignorance alike of European geography and economics and of the real nature of Communism.

It is in relation to the last point that this work, which is in no way political in nature or aim, may lay claim to make a contribution of decisive importance. It presents a view of Communism, which if true, has an urgent bearing on the present crisis, and which Americans and all free men must assimilate if they are to grasp the real peril in which the world stands.

My indebtedness to many people because of their interest and patience in listening to me as well as their active loyalty and support, is great. The Vestry and Congregation of All Saints' Church, Chevy Chase, have endured much, I am sure, but I receive at their hands only generosity and kindness. In particular, I have had much help, alike in counsel and in encouragement, from a brilliant younger scientist, Dr. John Tatum Cox, Jr., and from General Roscoe C. Wilson, of the United States Air Force. I am indebted to my close and dear friend, Bishop Donegan, for the hospitality the past summer of the pulpit of his great Cathedral of Saint John the Divine, New York City, and for his signal confidence in me and graciousness in allowing the present work to emerge under his patronage. To Mr. Clifford P. Morehouse, for long a friend and now my publisher, I am especially grateful. But for his persistence in telling me that I ought to write *this book*, it probably would never have materialized.

There are four colleagues and friends to whom I am deeply indebted. My Associate, the Reverend Charles H. Best, could not have shown more interest in a child of his own brain than he has in the present work. In every possible way he has sought to help, giving of himself unselfishly and beyond the call of duty to spare me in routine tasks. By his thoughtful criticism, also, and his generous appreciation he has contributed not a little to my own thought processes. Mrs. Mary H. McClain added to other voluntary labors for her Church the heavy burden of turning out the typescript of the entire book. Her willing effort, incomparable efficiency, and pride and enthusiasm in the undertaking have been a continual inspiration. Mrs. Edith W. Hood, my secretary for many years and the preserver of my office peace, has helped far more than she has any idea by her cheerful presence, entire reliability, and constant endeavor to make everything run easily and smoothly. Earlier this past year the labor of wrestling with the not always readily decipherable manuscript of a volume which had been projected on Democracy was voluntarily undertaken by my long-time colleague and friend, Mrs. Kate Rowe Holland. I remain none the less grateful to her, though her work has as yet borne no direct fruit.

In a number of instances, I have quoted passages from the *Revised Standard Version of the New Testament,* copyrighted in 1946 by the International Council of Religious Education, and published by Thomas Nelson & Sons, New York. These quotations are used by their permission.

CHARLES W. LOWRY

Chevy Chase, Maryland
Columbus Day
October 12, 1951

Contents

		PAGE
FOREWORD BY THE BISHOP OF NEW YORK		vii
PREFACE		ix
CHAPTER I. COMMUNISM—A NEW RELIGION		1
Origin of Socialism		2
Early Motives of Socialism		3
Influence of Plato and Rousseau		5
Marx and Marxism		6
Dialectical Explained		7
Examples of Dialectic		10
The Truth in Hegelian Dialectic		11
Dialectical Materialism a Contradiction		12
The Marxist System in Diagram Form		14
Brief Summary of Marxism		15
Economic Determinism		16
The Class Struggle		17
Marx the Believer		19
Marxism Becomes a Universal Religion		21
Lenin as Messiah		24
Lenin as a Realist		25
Differences from Marx		27
Stalin—Background and Character		29
Worship of Stalin		31
Revival of Imperialism		32
A New Tower of Babel		33
Conclusion		36
Tabular Comparison of Christianity and Communism		37

PAGE

CHAPTER II. THE BACKGROUND OF COMMUNISM . . . 39

Older Meaning of "Religion" 39
The Era before Christ 40
Religion and Faith 42
The Ancient Mystery Religions 43
Why Christianity Won Out 45
The West in a New Religious Phase 48
Signs and Evidences: Seven Fields of Fact 49
(1) Religious Revival 50
(2) The Thrust to the Sensate and the Sensual . . 55
(3) Insecurity—A Collective Neurosis 58
(4) The New Demons 61
(5) Psychiatry—A New Priesthood 65
(6) Existentialism: or Subjectivity in Rebound . . 69
(7) The Rise of a New World Religion 74
Summary 74
Menace and Promise 75

CHAPTER III. THE CHRISTIAN REVOLUTION 77

Christianity—A Spiritual Revolution 78
Love and New Being 79
Assertion of Love in Christ 80
The Rejection of Love 81
The Triumph of Love 82
Love and Death 83
Life—Affirmation of Christ 85
Gospel of the Resurrection 86
A Second Modern Query 86
A New Historical Man 88
Proof to Be Found in Greek Man 91

PAGE

Sense of Finiteness 92
Sense of Mortality 92
Dualism 94
Modern Faith in History 95
Democracy—Ancient and Modern 96
Totalitarian Reaction 99
Democracy as a Faith 99
Opportunity for America 100

CHAPTER IV. JESUS CHRIST AND THE AMERICAN WAY . 102

Democracy and Spiritual Renewal 103
Finality of Figure of Christ 104
Development Potential of Christianity 108
Democracy—A Segment of Christian
    Consciousness 109
Art as Mirror of History 111
Twentieth Century and Prodigal Son 112
Can Americans Wake Up? 114
Humility and Recovery 117
What Is the American Way? 118
Danger of Shallowness 121
A Fresh Evaluation 123
Christ and the American Way 125
(1) Life 126
(2) Liberty 129
Finality of Democracy 132
A Mixed Political Economy 133
Freedom Under God 135
(3) The Pursuit of Happiness 135
Love and Happiness 136
The Cross—The Inner Meaning of History . . . 138

PAGE

Chapter V. Communism and Christ 141

Three Examples of Religion 141
The Example of Communism 143
The October Club at Oxford 144
Why Communism Appeals 145
An Exuberant Materialism 146
Divorce of Reason and Love 148
Christian View of Reality 149
Doctrine that God Is Love 151
Practical Results of Christianity 155
Second Law of Human Nature 156
Antichrist 158
Power of a Dream 159
A Naked Realism 160
Code of Politburo 161
Radical Weakness of Communism 163
Assets of Christianity 165
Christianity and a Better World 168

Epilogue. Three Remarkable Prophecies 171

1. Heine on Germany, Communism, and
   Russia (1842) 171
2. De Tocqueville on Russia and the United
   States (1835) 172
3. Henry Adams on Russia and China (1903) . . 173

A Select Bibliography 175

I

Communism—a New Religion

And they said, Go to, let us build us a city,
and a tower, whose top may reach unto heaven.
—*Genesis 11:4.*

COMMUNISM is a form of socialism. By Communists it
is regarded *as* Socialism; there is not, and cannot be,
any other kind. This, of course, is a religious, not a scientific,
judgment, and is a good example of the dogmatic authori-
tarianism of Communism. Nevertheless, it is worth dwelling
upon the fact that both the founders and the modern leaders
of the latter are intensely Socialist in their consciousness,
and commonly use the terms Socialism and Communism as
interchangeable. Thus the Party is called Communist and
is so designated in the Soviet Constitution. The official name
of the new Russia is "the Union of Soviet Socialist Republics." This union is defined in the first article of the Soviet
Constitution (of 1936) as "a socialist state of workers and
peasants." Throughout the Constitution, with the one exception already noted, it is the phrase "Socialist" which is used,
generally in a context of contrast to capitalism.

It is clear, then, that there is a very close connection between Communism and Socialism and that the latter is the
older and original phrase. What was Socialism originally
and how did it arise?

Origin of Socialism

It arose as a result jointly of two strains of thought. The first was the liberal doctrine of man which underlay both the American and the French Revolutions. This doctrine did not emerge full-grown all at once; it is the doctrine of man made possible by Christianity but developed actually by the modern philosophers beginning with Descartes. For these thinkers and in time for most educated Europeans and Americans man is a rational being, a mind associated with a body, a free will endowed by nature and nature's God with the inalienable rights of liberty and equality. For John Locke as for George Mason in Virginia and many other Americans prior to 1776, property was also an inalienable natural right. This view was expressive of the fact that the liberal doctrine had developed hand in hand with mercantile capitalism. The withdrawal of property as one of the sacred human trinity, manifest in Jefferson and accepted generally by both the theorists and the practitioners of revolution in France a few years later, is a prophecy of the second strain of thought which combined with the first to produce Socialism.

The second strain is the reaction of thought and feeling evoked in an increasing number of Europeans by the inequalities and oppression resulting from the Industrial Revolution. This immensest and most radical of all revolutions since the discovery of fire, played havoc in its first phases with human values. In the feudal order the life of the producer, the serf, was meagre and brutish. But he was surrounded by safeguards and protections, derived from a sense of Christian responsibility and brotherly obligation and sanctified by custom from time immemorial. The meanest serf, in other words, had rights as clearly defined as the feudal lord in relation to other lords and to his sovereign king. With the freeing of the serfs abstract rights became greater but protection and security disappeared. With the appearance of risk capital and the boom in trade of all kinds, the cultivation of the soil especially in England became less extensive and the supply of labor more plentiful. Finally, with the appearance of machines this labor was readily absorbed and women and children were drawn into the labor market. The hours were long, as they had been on the land. But with the hours went appalling conditions of light, air, and sanitation and none of the compensations inherent in rural life. Worst of all, the employer commonly felt no sense of responsibility. The worker was a free agent. He did not have to work. Neither did the employer have to hire him. Labor became a commodity to be bought and sold mechanically and impersonally like any other commodity; and it was regulated like other goods by the law of supply and demand.

There was, to the everlasting credit of the human conscience, a loud outcry at the excesses and abuses of the Industrial Revolution. It seemed that its results denied the very principles upon which political democracy was founded and for which two Revolutions had been fought and won. How to reconcile these two contradictories: the absolute rights of liberty and equality, and the unqualified institution of private property?

EARLY MOTIVES OF SOCIALISM

The problem thus posed is not soluble without some alteration in the two terms. Socialism represents the radical step of calling for the abolition of the second term, private property, at least so far as the means of production and hence also risk capital are concerned. Its primal motivation was humanitarian, and in England in one important phase Christian. F. D. Maurice and Charles Kingsley are examples of pioneer Christian Socialism: A group of Churchmen inspired by Maurice were arranging, at the very time of Marx's arrival in London, to issue a new set of *Tracts For Priests and People*. In 1854 they founded the Working Men's College in Red Lion Square, London. Robert Owen (1771-1858), who anticipated them by nearly half a century, was a Deist. For lofty humanitarianism he has never been excelled. Here are three or four sentences from his *Letters to the Human Race on the Coming Universal Revolution*.

Any religion that does not produce in practice, universal truth, justice, charity or love, among the whole family of man is spurious—is of no value to the human race. . . .

Happiness can be attained only by the united feelings of charity and love among the entire population of the world. . . .

Charity and love for our race can emanate only from a correct knowledge of the laws of humanity relative to the formation of man. . . .

This is that religion of truth, honesty, and common-sense, which the rational system of society can and will produce over the world.

By this rational system Owen means the abolition of competition and the profit system, and just and beneficial distribution of wealth for all through its just and beneficial creation by all. His reasoning is simple and clear. It moves from the religion of reason, the universal natural religion of rational man, to the renunciation of a system which is irrational and which contradicts the universal principles of charity and love.

In France the first Socialists reasoned along similar if less idealistically stated lines. The great emphasis of the Revolution had been on equality. If this is applied economically, it follows that property must be owned and production directed socially or by the state, so that all may share equally. Such is the essential reasoning of figures like Babeuf, Saint-Simon, Fourier, and the anarchist Proudhon, who both influenced Marx and attacked him in one of the most trenchant and devastating criticisms of Communism ever made.

INFLUENCE OF PLATO AND ROUSSEAU

These two factors, the liberal view of man and humanitarian reaction against industrialism, are sufficient to account for the rise of Socialism. In addition, two other influences may be noted, Plato and Rousseau. The sociology of Maurice not less than his theology was deeply influenced by Plato. The same was true of a great English Archbishop, William Temple, nearly a century later. The Greek understanding of man, society, and the state is quite different from that of modern individualistic liberalism. Man is considered a social being, a political animal, who needs the State in a positive sense for his own development and virtuous upbringing. Justice can only be realized generally in the lives of individuals if it is first the ideal and goal of the State. Plato and Aristotle have for generations been central in the curriculum of the ancient English universities, Oxford and Cambridge, and this has without doubt been an important factor in the unique victory in England of Fabian Socialism.[1]

[1] By Fabian Socialism is meant a gradual or evolutionary point of view with respect to the coming of the Socialist State. The Fabian Society was founded in 1884 by a group of English Socialists who were opposed to immediate revolutionary action. The word Fabian is from the name of a celebrated Roman leader, Quintus Fabius Maximus, who received the surname Cunctator or "Delayer" for his success with delaying tactics against Hannibal in the Second Punic War.

As for Rousseau, the extreme yet typical Romanticist, he has influenced everyone who has come after him. What Rousseau did was to let typical Liberalism go, and emphasize in a naturalized secular fashion the older Christian view of redeemed man. Thus he accents the community, the general will, brotherhood, and love. We might say that he socializes man on a naturalistic basis. Man is naturally kind, fraternal, good. He is the victim of the entrenched evils of society perpetuated by the power of tradition and corrupt vested interests. By the reform of society, it follows, all things can be accomplished. Man can regain his true image, and can become as virtuous in civilization as he was once noble amid savage and primitive surroundings.

Marx and Marxism

It is evident that the logic of Rousseau's view is such as to give a strong impetus to Socialism. We can see a very similar thing happen in the case of Karl Marx. Convinced not only of the truth of Socialism but also that it is inevitably coming, he proceeds to naturalize the Christian doctrine of the Kingdom of God and to identify it with the ultimate, surely predictable, rationally necessary Socialist Utopia. Here is the root of Communism in its religious aspect. Here is the explanation of its transformation into a fantastic world religion of salvation. Marx, however, had no idea that this was what he was doing. His intention as an analyst and prophet was something quite different.

Marx was a baptized German Jew, who espoused the idealist philosophy of Hegel in his university days, was converted to materialism by Ludwig Feuerbach, became a Socialist under the influence of Proudhon, and undertook as his life work the elaboration of a scientific foundation for Socialism. This sounds a little like the nursery jingle, "The

Farmer Takes a Wife," but it is a fairly accurate summary of the transitions of his restless mind and life. The great Lenin in his authoritative work *The Teachings of Karl Marx* gives this summary of the master:

> Marx was the genius who continued and completed the three chief ideological currents of the nineteenth century, represented respectively by the three most advanced countries of humanity: classical German philosophy, classical English political economy, and French socialism combined with French revolutionary doctrines.[2]

What Lenin failed to include and would have denied with vehemence, is the unconscious ethical passion derived by Marx from his Semitic inheritance and the equally unrecognized faith in history despite and because of suffering which he received from Christianity. Or to put it more briefly, Lenin failed to include Marx's unconscious attempt to continue and complete the Biblical doctrine of the Kingdom of God. *Without this fourth strain, however, Marxism would never have become the religion of Communism.*

We turn now to a more detailed exposition of Marxism or the teachings of Karl Marx. This will be followed by a survey of the contributions of Lenin and Stalin, and the evolution of Communism under their leadership. Finally, we shall consider and attempt to dissect the anatomy of the developed, living, advancing religion of Communism, seeking to understand its appeal, to estimate its peril, and to point out its vulnerability.

DIALECTICAL EXPLAINED

The first doctrine of Marx is dialectical materialism. It underlies all other Communist teachings. By dialectical, which he derived from Hegel, is meant the constant move-

[2] From V. I. Lenin, *Selected Works* (Moscow, Foreign Language Publishing House).

ment and change of objects, so that one thing or process is changed into its opposite and that in turn is transformed into still something else. From this it follows that the world-order is not something static and inflexible, but fluid and capable of evolution. Lenin, in the work already cited, quotes from Engels, friend of Marx and co-author of the *Communist Manifesto* of 1848, a beautifully lucid explanation of dialectical.

The great basic idea that the world is not to be viewed as a complex of fully fashioned objects, but as a complex of processes, in which apparently stable objects, no less than the images of them inside our heads (our concepts), are undergoing incessant changes, arising here and disappearing there, and which with all apparent accident and in spite of all momentary retrogression, ultimately constitutes a progressive development—this great basic idea has, particularly since the time of Hegel, so deeply penetrated the general consciousness that hardly any one will now venture to dispute it in its general form. *But it is one thing to accept it in words, quite another thing to put it in practice on every occasion and in every field of investigation.*[3]

One might wonder, why on every occasion or in every field, or why it is necessary to posit anything regular, law-abiding, or inevitably progressive, since what is being defined is the behavior of matter and matter alone. This question Marxists have never answered, for it is unanswerable. The truth, of course, is that Hegelians of all kinds were busy applying the dialectical formula to history, and Marx and Engels saw a brilliant opportunity to advance Socialism by exhibiting it as an example of dialectical necessity. Material-ism they had embraced not because it fitted Hegelian

[3] Lenin, *op. cit.*

dialectic, but because they wanted to or felt compelled to on other grounds. There is some evidence that Marx was interested in materialism and was in rebellion emotionally against God and all conventional religion before he came strongly under the influence of Feuerbach. Indeed it seems possible that the latter's atheism and extreme doctrine of projectionism [or the view that religion is a projection of man's self-feeling and self-consciousness] made a stronger appeal than his materialism to the frustrated and embittered young intellectual.

For Hegel, as for Plato at the dawn of philosophy, dialectic is a mental operation and development. It is the way truth is discovered and rendered living and effective for the experiencing, thinking subject. In Plato's *Dialogues* (compare *dialectic*) Socrates gets round to the statement of what is true and good only after many engagements with opposing points of view. Sometimes he adopts himself for a moment some of these standpoints. In the end, and after the most thorough discussion of thesis and counter-thesis, he reaches what he asserts, and Plato believes, is the truth.

Hegel carried the idea of dialectic much further. For him, too, it is and remains a mental operation. *It is the logic of God.* It is the way the Divine Mind moves and is fulfilled in nature and history. Man, who is in God and God in him, is only thinking the Divine thought when he thinks correctly.

But Hegel did a second thing with dialectic. He claimed for it a steady, unvarying pattern. It is the way thought takes place, and thought always moves first by advancing an idea. This idea or thesis suggests or begets its opposite. Then out of the contradiction springs a reconciliation in a larger idea or synthesis.

Examples of Dialectic

This is the famed theory of thesis, antithesis, and synthesis. A simple example would be: The experience of tyranny begets a desire for freedom; freedom, however, easily turns into license, and needs to find true expression in the larger synthesis of ordered liberty, or government by constitution, or free individual acceptance of discipline and restraint.

A second example was made much of by a Church historian named Baur who taught at Tübingen in Germany and applied Hegelian dialectic on a large scale to the development in history of Christian ideas and institutions. Christianity began as a movement within Judaism and accepted without question the full law of Moses. This was found stifling and unsatisfactory, and so a St. Paul arises to proclaim the end of the Law and the fullness of Christian Liberty. This doctrine is equally one-sided and tends to end in antinomianism or lawless immoral excess. So St. John proclaims a new commandment of love and the rising Holy Catholic Church reaffirms the moral aspect of Mosaic law even as it abolishes the ceremonial part and stresses Christian freedom in contrast to the older bondage.

Still a third example might be the spirit of independence generated in the American colonies as a result jointly of geographical isolation with indefinite room to expand and the irritating exaction of taxes by a far away Mother country. This new spirit found expression in the successful Revolutionary War, in rabid stress on freedom and equality, and in the idea of as little government and that as local as possible. This produced many excesses and made social cohesion and prosperity impossible. The result was powerful Federalist and centralist reaction, with serious proposals by

Hamilton of New York, a gallant patriot, John Adams of Massachusetts, and many others to found monarchical government in America. In the end this extreme contradiction of the Revolution gave rise to the fertile synthesis of the Constitution of the United States of America, with the Bill of Rights included as Amendment I. It is noteworthy that the principal architects of the Constitution were the arch-conservative Hamilton and the liberal conservative Madison, and that the whole enterprise was resented and opposed by the unreconstructed liberal, Thomas Jefferson.

THE TRUTH IN HEGELIAN DIALECTIC

Evidently, we have in Hegel's theory of dialectic a very fruitful and suggestive principle—one that illuminates our understanding of past and present, and may guide us in thinking about the future. It is evident too that our minds work this way, perhaps because in experience we do tend to extremes and have to learn through awakening to hard consequences the wisdom of inclusiveness and balance.

Hegel, however, claimed for his trinal dialectical principle universal application and absolute validity. It supplies the key to nature and all history. It unlocks the mystery of self-consciousness—of subject, object, and their union in self-aware personality; and resolves finally the age-long incomprehensibility of the Trinitarian nature of God. God's own being and consciousness are dialectical: He is idea or subject; He goes out in finite contradiction to Himself as object in nature and history (this is the creation); and this relative opposition is overcome in the synthesis of Absolute Spirit, which is God's perfect self-consciousness, self-realization, and Transcendent Eternity. It is interesting to speculate that the ultimate source of Hegelianism is the Christian doctrine of the Trinity, just as the primal root of Marxism is the Biblical idea of the Kingdom of God.

Anyway, Hegel took his dialectical discovery with complete seriousness, and Marx follows him here without deviation. Reality is dialectical. But with the help of Feuerbach, also of the left-wing Hegelian group, and encouraged by his example in turning inside out and upside down the master's seamless robe of universal reality, Marx took the decisive step of making spirit something purely derivative, simply an incidental effect, and saying, Matter is all. He was also able to say, anticipating Friedrich Nietzsche by several decades, God is dead. One gets the impression that Marx, re-enforced by Feuerbach's religious analysis, reached this conclusion with a certain vehemence of satisfaction, in marked contrast to Nietzsche's air of tragic regret and strained desperate melancholy.

DIALECTICAL MATERIALISM A CONTRADICTION

Reality then is matter. History is bread. A man is what he eats. But matter behaves dialectically; it behaves just exactly like Hegel's spirit incarnating itself in material form; mysteriously but certainly it advances by the ever recurring pattern of thesis, antithesis, and synthesis. Furthermore, *the* philosopher knows how the development is now continuing and how in the future it will move on to the final goal—to full fruition and perfection. *The* philosopher now, however, is Marx, not Hegel, and I believe that Marx now goes his former master one better, revealing his Jewishness in contrast to the Germanic mentality of the other. Hegel, it is true, glorified the Prussian state and suggested that in its unification and advance the Absolute was present and moving toward some wonderful realization. But this is in the realm of speculation; it is a sort of metaphysical effervescence; it is an expression of the irresistible Teutonic impulse to self-reverence and self-glorification. It is not sober philosophizing and it is in no way essential to the system.

With Marx the reverse is true. *The intuition of the future is of the essence of the system.* He ceases in reality to be a philosopher and becomes a prophet. He ceases to speculate; he affirms and predicts. The form and content are very different, but the spirit is that of the old prophets of Israel: "Thus saith the Lord; it shall surely come to pass." Matter is God; his omnipotent word by which the heavens and the earth are made to be remade, is Dialectic; and Karl Marx, the great, bushy-bearded, dark "Moor" of Soho, is his prophet.

It makes, of course, no sense. It never made any sense. The system of Marx and Marxism is a structure riven from top to bottom by a gaping, glaring contradiction. But Marx was not one to be stopped by this. He was driven by passion, by hatred, by identification in his own sense of rejection with the rejected proletariat of this world, by desire to change drastically the world, by the need of faith. Contradiction never yet stopped a virile faith. "I believe," thundered Tertullian of Africa, "because it is impossible."

Marx would have shuddered at the very idea of possible classification with an irrational obscurantist like Tertullian. He was a philosopher, a scientist, an economist. Truth, facts, inevitabilities spoke for themselves. So he assumed, and was never disillusioned. The Marxists since have done the same. He held on to Dialectical Materialism as to life itself. All Marxists do the same. If they did not, the whole house would fall. It is the foundation-faith, the keystone of the dogmatic arch, the construct of the Ultimately Real. From it all else

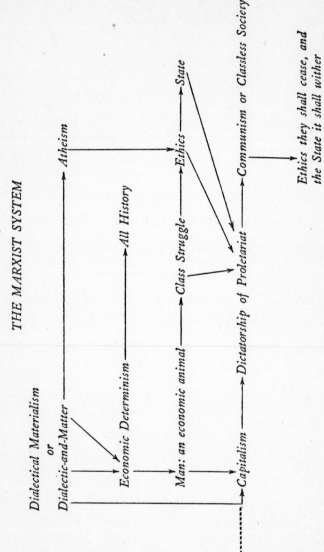

THE MARXIST SYSTEM

Dialectical Materialism
or
Dialectic-and-Matter

Atheism

All History

Economic Determinism

Man: an economic animal

Class Struggle

Ethics

State

Capitalism

Dictatorship of Proletariat

Communism or Classless Society

Ethics they shall cease, and the State it shall wither away!

Supreme Example of Thesis, Antithesis, and Synthesis

follows. It is to Communism what Brahma, the All, is to Hinduism, and what the living God is in the Bible and to Christians.

The relation of all other Marxist doctrines to Dialectical Materialism and to one another is portrayed graphically in

---

BRIEF SUMMARY OF MARXISM EXPLAINING DIAGRAM ON OPPOSITE PAGE

The foundation doctrine is Dialectical Materialism. It is more accurate to say Dialectic-and-Matter, for the Dialectic was taken from Hegel's Idealism and its combination with Matter only is most arbitrary. Atheism follows directly from Matter.

Applied to history Dialectical Materialism means Economic Determinism. Dialectic is very important here, for the Determinism involves progress and a final goal. Economics determines all things historical, including man's consciousness and conduct. For economic man class struggle is unavoidable and central. It determines all ethics and explains the origin and function of the state. The present phase of history is the culmination of developing economic forces.

Capitalism is organized greed. It is economic man amassing great wealth through technical mastery and the exploitation of the helpless proletariat. But it begets its own negation, for the workers, growing ever more miserable and discontented, will rise in revolution and forcibly seize the power of the state. This period of Dictatorship, the antithesis of liberal democracy, is only temporary, for once private ownership is abolished the basis for the existence of classes, class struggle, and the state disappears. Thus inevitably there follows the synthesis of Communist or Classless Society.

the Diagram found on page 14. On the facing page 15, in italicised type, the Diagram is explained and the Marxist system summarized in a few sentences.

ECONOMIC DETERMINISM

The second basic teaching of Marx follows directly from his materialism. It is economic determinism or the view that all history and all culture—all human reality—is at base economic. Economics is at the center of history: *it is matter in historical form*. This doctrine is summed up in a concise, packed sentence of the *Communist Manifesto*:

In every historical epoch the prevailing mode of economic production and exchange, and the social organization necessarily following from it, form the basis upon which it is built up, and from which alone can be explained, the political and intellectual history of that epoch.[4]

But it is not merely history in the broadest sense, in its main currents and trends, in its politics and philosophy, that is economically determined. It is, also, man himself—man in the marrow and fibre of his existence, man in the full extent and totality of his interests and achievements. Man is an economic animal. He is not determined by anything inherent in himself but by his environment, his social existence. And this in turn is the reflex of conditions of production and exchange. As Marx put it, in a passage quoted by Lenin and by many other students and analysts of Marxism:

The mode of production of the material means of life determines, in general, the social, political, and intellectual processes of life. It is not the consciousness of human beings that determines their existence, but, conversely, it is their social existence that determines their consciousness.[5]

[4] Marx, *op. cit.*, Preface.
[5] Preface, *A Contribution to the Critique of Political Economy*.

This doctrine of man as essentially a social product, a being determined by environment and not a given nature, is momentous for Marxism. It after all is a proposal to transform history and nature. This explains the touchiness of Communist leaders, who are bound to be theorists, at least in the lower brackets, in fields like biology and genetics. In the free world wheat is wheat, and peas are peas. The Mendelian law is true, or it is not. Let the evidence speak for itself. Who cares really whether Lamarck or Darwin was right? The only issue is which one is supported by the facts. But for Marxism, which like all orthodoxies is a tight interlocked logical structure, there can be no truce with heresy at any point. Pull out one or two stones and the whole edifice may crumble.

THE CLASS STRUGGLE

The Marxist view of man, which is the expression of materialism and economic determinism, is expressed, in turn, in the theory of the class struggle and in a class interpretation of both ethics and the state. All history, says Marx in the *Communist Manifesto,* is the history of class struggles. The classes are two, oppressor and oppressed. Always they have "carried on perpetual warfare, sometimes masked, sometimes open and acknowledged." The great mark of bourgeois society is its simplification of class antagonisms, its setting man against man according to the law of his economic interest. More and more in this society the battle-line is sharpened. It is the bourgeoisie—the haves—against the proletariat—the have-nots—and vice versa. In this situation lies the world's hope, for the only revolutionary class is the proletariat, the unpropertied, the dispossessed. They and they alone will fight the capitalists, for their interest is clear and unmistakable. They have nothing to lose.

What is ethics? It is entirely ideological; it is the rationalization of class interest. The perception of the omnipresence of the class struggle and its critical importance for the outcome of history, leads to a radical revaluation of values. It provides the only ethical norm there can be. The good is the advancement of the proletariat as the chosen people of history. Right conduct is always and under all circumstances that which assists revolution, the overthrow of capitalism, the dictatorship of the proletariat, and the coming eventually of pure Communism. No means whatever are barred; there is no good nor bad in methods, but only problems of judgment. The sole consideration is assisting most effectively the cause of proletarian revolution.

Equally clear-cut is the Marxist view of the state. It is not an order of nature, but a product of oppression. It is not an arrangement required by the general welfare, but the result of class war. It is, in Lenin's words, interpreting Marx and Engels, "the product and the manifestation of the *irreconcilability* of class antagonisms." It arises out of the self-protective instinct of society when social conflict grows too painful to bear. Its essence is power over society with its conflicts—the power of armies, of police, of courts, of taxation. Power, however, must be wielded by some one, and it generally happens that an alliance is formed, openly or covertly, between those who bear rule and the most powerful classes economically. In the bourgeois period this has been increasingly the case. Capitalism by an inherent necessity increases both the number and the misery of the proletariat. It must, as tension mounts and violent action is threatened, rely more and more on the power of the State. Similarly but vice versa, the proletariat must do the same if and when it comes to power. It must take over the state and make use of its instrumentalities during the period of transition from revolution to full Communism.

MARX THE BELIEVER

This brings us, finally, to Marx's teaching that history is in its final dialectical phase, and that this phase consists of capitalism as thesis, the dictatorship of the proletariat as antithesis, and Communism or a classless society as synthesis. We reach here the heart of the Communist analysis and faith. We see Marx the scientific economist and Marx the believer. The advantage of Dialectic was that it permitted and assisted under the guise of seeming rationalism the union of facts and faith. We touch here the appeal of Marxism to contemporary man caught in the contradictions of the vast impersonal system of industrialism, unsure of the future of a confused and confusing world, and deprived of "the certain hope of immortality," which as late as the eighteenth century was a cardinal tenet of rational religion.

Marx was not an acute or original philosopher. He was a very elementary historian. He was not a logician or a psychologist. From all these angles his system is shot through with holes. But he was an economist, who worked indefatigably and who attempted to continue, correct, and complete the work of the classical British economists. It was in this connection and with the aim of scientific mastery that he slaved away year after year in the British Museum and brought forth the monumental work destined to become because of its erudition and scientific claim the Bible of Communism, *Das Kapital* or *Capital*.

It is not possible here to go into the use made by Marx of

the classical distinction between *value in use* and *value in exchange,* or of his special theory of *surplus-value,* or of his division of total capital into *constant capital* and *variable capital.*[6] It is sufficient to say that he combined in his attemptedly exhaustive study of Capitalism a vast array of facts with fertile theoretical ingenuity. If the classical concept of *laissez faire* had remained unmodified in economic practice and capitalists had proven to be purely economic men, unaffected by any non-economic considerations, Marx without doubt would have been infallible in his science and precise in the predictions based upon it. As it was, he miscalculated nearly everything, and incredible dexterity has been required on the part of Marxian theorists and Communist leaders in order to preserve and maintain his intellectual integrity and his validity as the source of orthodox truth. To give only two examples, the Revolution should have occurred in Germany or possibly Great Britain or the United States. The last place it was supposed to occur, on Marxist premises and predictions, was imperial, Czarist, backward, non-industrial, peasant Russia. This presented the Marxists with a poser.

The other example is the American adaptation of Capitalism, its ingenuity in meeting and surmounting new problems, its acceptance of one qualification after another of *laissez faire* theory, and the extraordinary prosperity and power to which the United States has risen. The truth, of course, is that man is infinitely adaptable and that history is replete with instances of Herbert Spencer's definition of tragedy—an idea slain by a fact. Karl Marx as a theorist definitely and incontrovertibly belongs in this category and historical museum.

[6] An admirable, brief, but thoroughly informed discussion of Marx's economic theory will be found in John H. Hallowell's *Main Currents in Modern Political Thought* (New York, Henry Holt & Co.), pp. 418 ff.

The same nemesis without doubt awaits the other stages of the supreme example in Marx's eyes of the truth of Dialectic, namely, the inevitable but temporary dictatorship of the proletariat, coming as a consequence of the rottenness and contradiction of Capitalism, and its equally necessary and infallibly predictable sequel, the dawn of universal Communism defined as the abolition or simple cessation of classes, class antagonism, and the state itself. Here, of course, Marx is no longer a scientist, in any sense. He supposes himself to be an Hegelian logician, but in reality he is a revert to Old Testament and New Testament prophecy. He is a man of faith, albeit an avowed atheist.

And he shall judge among many people, and rebuke strong nations afar off; and they shall beat their swords into ploughshares, and their spears into pruninghooks: nation shall not lift up a sword against nation, neither shall they learn war any more.

But they shall sit every man under his vine and under his fig tree; and none shall make them afraid.[7]

If any man have an ear, let him hear.

He that leadeth into captivity shall go into captivity: he that killeth with the sword must be killed with the sword. Here is the patience and the faith of the saints. . . .

And I saw a new heaven and a new earth: for the first heaven and the first earth were passed away. . . .

And God shall wipe away all tears from their eyes; and there shall be no more death, neither sorrow, nor crying, neither shall there be any more pain: for the former things are passed away.[8]

MARXISM BECOMES A UNIVERSAL RELIGION

It is this faith, manifest as such ambiguously and indirectly in Marx's vagueness in treating of the antithesis and still

[7] Micah 4:3, 4.
[8] Revelation 13:9, 10; 21:1, 4.

more of the synthesis, as compared with the precision and exactitude of his analysis of Capitalism, which secured the future of Communism and is the secret still of its contemporary appeal and power. The appeal of Marxism was, and is two-fold. It exploited, and exploits, the prestige of science, claiming to be a scientific system for a scientific age. It offered, and offers, deliverance from present injustice and misery, promising to all believers a new world of equality and happiness. This gospel of deliverance comes directly to the poor and dispossessed; to the uneasy and idealistic children of privilege it brings vicarious absolution from guilt and participation in righteousness.

The miracle of Marxism is not Marx, and is not his system —which as a whole is a crazy quilt of clashing colors, a weak patchwork of ill-fitting pieces, a conglomeration of ideas hammered into the most tenuous unity and possessing only a plausible and thin intellectual respectability. The miracle of Marxism is its social and institutional embodiment and its transformation into an aggressive, universal religion of salvation.

This is the miracle of every religion that passes the examinations of power and gains the accreditation of universality. The critical point, the crucial stage, is always the passage from idea, in the mind and heart of a founder, to embodiment in institution, in visible forms and ceremonies, in sacrament and cult, in systematized creed and code, in the adherence of growing multitudes of believers.

The case of Buddhism is instructive and is in some ways closely parallel. The Buddha, who happened to be a prince, had a tremendous idea. "The heavy and the weary weight of all this unintelligible" and purposeless world, could be lifted. It was not inevitable and unending. It was all owing to the obsession of desire. By its resolute surrender, by giving up the passionate will to live, to propagate, to acquire property, to gain power, and by turning to compassion for all suffering, the individual self can escape the wheel inexorable of sin and retribution, of life, death and rebirth, called Karma. It can enter into the peace and rest of an eternal calm. It can gain Nirvana.

Such was primitive original Buddhism. It resembles Marxism in the naive simplicity of its diagnosis of the human problem and in its dismissal of theology. There is also some similarity, though it is a veiled likeness, in the place of compassion in the Buddha's outlook. For Marx there is a blazing passion because of injustice, an identification with the rejected and helpless of this harsh world, which breaks forth occasionally in the cold, deliberate analysis of facts to which as a scientist he set himself. The Buddha says, here is the universe and its law; here is man; here is the answer. Marx did much the same, allowing for the fact of a scientific age and an industrial civilization. He, too, is atheistic. God is not in the picture. The world simply is. Buddhism did not become a world religion, however, until it was vastly altered and enlarged. The Absolute of Hinduism had to be picked up. The Buddha as the Compassionate One had to be deified and enthroned as the first of a succession of Saviours, coming into the world to minister to suffering mankind. Prayer is made to God through him. Rituals, temples, priests, the traditional apparatus of Oriental religion, make their appearance. Even so the new religion never took root in ancient, religion-sated India, but had to emigrate Northward and Eastward and Southward to assert its spiritual sway.

One could go on to compare Christianity and Mohammedanism, each differing from all others and in many respects unique, yet each showing a broadly similar development and making its real conquests not in the land of its origin but among new peoples. The same situation in a modern setting has come about before our eyes. The faith of Marxism, born in Germany, developed in Great Britain, with a scattering of cosmopolitan converts throughout Europe, moved Eastward, and in an ancient, backward nation of peasants fired a revolutionary flame, annexed and started in to transform a social system with the almost unlimited potential power of the Russian state, and has continued to expand and gain converts ever since. Today it has secured China and threatens all Asia. In every Western nation it has adherents and some zealous missionaries; in some it is a leading political, social, and intellectual factor.

To whom, to what, is this astounding development due? To Marx, the founder, in part. To the power of his faith. To the fulness of the time—its spiritual decay, its fear, its sense of contradiction, its feeling of entrapment in the grip of overwhelming impersonal forces, its unsatisfied hunger of soul. To various chances and networks of circumstance. But none or all of these are sufficient to account for the outcome—the present day religion of Communism.

The growth and spread of the new faith is the work primarily of two quite different, extraordinarily able men—Russians both and from their youth Marxist revolutionaries. Both renamed themselves—was it as a sign of conversion and new life?—and are known to history as Lenin and Stalin.

LENIN AS MESSIAH

Lenin is the eldest son of his spiritual father Marx and is the Messiah of Communism. His was the deed of revolution. He made the dream a reality, translated Scripture into fact, and brought about the incarnation of the proletarian Word in a social system. He, above all Marxists, was ready when the hour of destiny struck. He was ready, also, as unquestioned leader to interpret boldly and, if necessary, divide liberally the Word of Marxist truth, holding that "new occasions teach new duties" and require prudence and patience in applying first principles to the consolidation and extension of revolution. The symbol of Lenin's abiding presence in the new religion and in Socialist Russia, is his tomb in the Red Square of the Kremlin in Moscow and the perpetual cult of his body.

Marx had been concerned with the existing order, Capitalism. Lenin's task was the transition of the second, "antithetical" stage, the period of "the dictatorship of the proletariat." While an ardent Marxist and an undeviating proponent of scriptural orthodoxy on the new basis, Lenin could not afford to be vague. He had to make decisions. He had to act in complex and dangerous circumstances. Accordingly, he did not hesitate to supplement or artfully reinterpret Marx.

Lenin as a Realist

The first issue with which Lenin as a revolutionary leader had to deal, was the continuing role of force. Once the revolution was in being, there was an element which called for conciliation and deprecated persistence in violence and the execution of adversaries. The problem was complicated by the teaching of Marx and Engels on "the withering away of the state."

Lenin tackles this issue in his *Class Society and the State* (1917) from a broad angle but with a ferocious realism. "It is clear that the liberation of the oppressed class is impossible, not only without a violent revolution, *but also without the destruction* of the apparatus of state power which was created by the ruling class."[9] There must be no confusion of Marxism with opportunism, no slurring over of the necessity of violent, bloody revolution by invoking the doctrine of "the withering away of the state." The two points are clear and distinct; they can only be combined into an evolutionary single doctrine by the most unprincipled selection of texts and the substitution of eclecticism for dialectics.

The substitution of the proletarian state for the bourgeois state is impossible without a violent revolution. The abolition of the proletarian, i.e. of the state in general, is impossible except through the process of "withering away."[10]

Lenin, then, explores with great thoroughness and canny caution the period of transition from Capitalism to Communism in which, as Marx said, "the state can be nothing but the revolutionary dictatorship of the proletariat." He is clear that even in this period when Communism is coming to be, first, in the "lower" phase when it still bears the birthmarks of the old society, and, second, in the "higher" phase when in Marx's glowing words there shall no longer be any division of labor and "therewith the antithesis of mental and physical labor has vanished," it will be necessary to proceed slowly and on a carefully empirical basis.

That is why we have a right to speak only of the inevitable withering away of the state; we must emphasize the protracted nature of this process and its dependence upon the rapidity of development of the *higher phase* of communism; and we leave the question of length of time, or the concrete forms of the withering

[9] Lenin, *op. cit.*
[10] Lenin, *op. cit.*

away, quite open, because *no material is available* to enable us to answer these questions.[11]

So far it is not a question of revising Marx but of interpreting his theories in the face of concrete political responsibility. It would be fair to say, however, that the Leninist interpretation tempers the idealism and glow of the founder's dream. The movement is toward realism.

Differences from Marx

In at least three respects, the statesman took up or had earlier taken up a different position from the theorist-founder. The most critical was with respect to the active role of the proletariat. Marx had believed that it was only necessary for Capitalism to persist, with its inner contradictions growing ever more acute. The proletariat would automatically increase in class-consciousness, and would finally and spontaneously unite to throw off the yoke. *Lenin saw that this was not happening and would not happen.* Therefore, he said, the workers could not be left to their own efforts and their own natural "trade-union consciousness." They must be aroused, educated, and led from the outside. There must be an organ for this purpose, there must be a "revolutionary vanguard," there must be a Communist Party. *In this Party would be vested when revolution came, the dictatorship of the proletariat.*

This was a development of far-reaching significance. In addition, it was a serious deviation from Marx and what was universally regarded as orthodox Marxism and scientific socialism. A distinguished theorist, Plekhanov, highly praised at an earlier time by Lenin, described this break with Marx

[11] Lenin, *op. cit.*

and Marxists as "his [Lenin's] enormous mistake, his theoretical fall into sin."[12]

Lenin is the founder of the idea and reality of the revolutionary Party. It is the Church of political religion. In this development Leninism represents a swing from democracy to aristocracy and potential autocracy.

Lenin was more nationalist than his master. Or it would perhaps be more accurate to say simply that he was much less an internationalist. This led him to the two other differences with Marx. He broke with the view expressed in the *Communist Manifesto* that the peasants are reactionary and negative from the standpoint of solidarity with the proletariat. He believed their discontent could be utilized and against Marx, also, opposed immediate collectivization of the land.

Similar in motive is the last difference we shall note, namely, Lenin's tactic of encouraging national revolts everywhere as a way of weakening Capitalism and the bourgeois order directly. Partly the motive here is primary concern with revolution in Russia, *and we have in Leninism the seed of the coming resurgence of Russian nationalism as an aspect of Communism.* Partly also, one suspects, it is cold reason and practical realism as against a purer faith in the unassisted processes of Dialectic.

Does this mean any lessening of the religious drive and faith-aspect of Communism? On the contrary, Lenin was not only made a god from the standpoint of adulation, worship, and cult. He was elevated to the Pantheon alongside Marx as scientist and legislator. The sacred Canon was extended to include his writings. They became the New Testament of Communism. Party members were expected to

---

[12] Quoted by Hallowell, *op. cit.,* p. 492.

master not Marxism but the principles of Marxism-Leninism. Today the Chinese Mao speaks never simply of Marxism but of Marxism-Leninism or of Marxist-Leninist science.

STALIN—BACKGROUND AND CHARACTER

The third great figure of Communism is Stalin. In some respects he is the most interesting, as he is certainly the most enigmatic, of the triumvirate. Karl Marx was a German Jew, a philosopher, an idealist, an internationalist. He regarded himself as the secretary of humanity. Lenin was the son of a government official, a university man, a lawyer. He was a European Russian, with a mind like a rapier, an intellectual to his finger-tips, but with a strong sense of reality. Stalin is an Asiatic, a child of poverty, a peasant one generation removed from serfdom. He was not highly educated but was influenced by a pious mother, and perhaps his poverty, to enter a theological seminary. It is notable that his early revolutionary writings reflect the imagery of the Bible. His mind was on the slow side, thorough rather than brilliant. One has the sense in him always of the cunning of the peasant.

It has been said of Stalin that in his Socialism there was not a trace of a sense of guilt. The same student of the lord of all Russians observes that class hatred "was not his second nature—it was his first." These statements, which of course have in mind his background and origins, tell us a great deal about Stalin. They are perhaps the key to a cold ruthlessness, in which deep temperament has added a quality all its own to the experience of a revolutionary agitator and to thorough indoctrination with the ideas of Lenin. It was a Kulak who saw without flinching ten million Kulaks starve as a result of non-coöperation in the collectivization of their

land. It was a heart of iron that could say to the Polish
General Sikorsky, interceding for his countrymen: "Why
do you protest that there are 1,500,000 Poles in Siberia? I
have 12,000,000 Russians there." Perhaps, also, only some one
born at the very bottom of the social ladder and carrying
within the depths of his soul a fierce whirlpool of inferiority,
could lap up without nausea the religious adulation and
never ending extravaganza of personal flattery poured out
on the Russian leader from every side.

Stalin came to power in 1927. He has already reigned
twenty-four years, as compared with Lenin's less than seven.
He set out from Lenin's position, which of course does not
mean he is non-Marxist. There is considerable evidence that
he is a convinced Marxist so far as main lines are concerned
and that his foreign policy since 1945 has been in part
determined by the expectation of calamitous deterioration in
the American capitalistic system. He set out from and has
continued Lenin's highly practical interpretation of the spirit
of Marxism. He himself has made no contribution to theory.
He proceeds from both his great precursors but adds nothing
on his own.

What Stalin has done is to be the presiding genius of the
Soviet Communist system for a quarter of a century, direct-
ing the ship of state and the ark of the Party-Church through
consolidation of political power, ambitious programs for in-
creased industrialization, greater production, and collectivization of agriculture, military battle for survival, and
renewed missionary activity on a world scale, accompanied
by all the tricks of propaganda and infiltration. In policy
he has been ultra-cautious, quick to purge the party and
army of opposition, pliant as an interpreter of Marxist truth
when a practical issue arises like opening the Churches as

a war morale-measure, given to reliance upon vast inequality of rewards as the rather peculiar cement of a society on the way to becoming classless.

WORSHIP OF STALIN

On the wide front of general analysis, three Stalinist developments seem gravely significant. The first is the virtual deification of Stalin in his own lifetime and the elaboration of a definite cult for his worship and praise. This may be a deliberate design for holding the miserable masses by drawing toward the living leader the unchanged religious ardor of the Russian soul. It certainly reflects a shift from Party rule in some real sense (Lenin: for Marx it had been rule of the proletariat) to the absolute rule of a single will. Here is a hymn to Stalin of extraordinary fervor and beauty, reminding one of Eastern Byzantine Christianity in the fourth and following centuries.

> O great Stalin, O leader of the peoples,
> Thou who broughtest man to birth,
> Thou who purifiest the earth,
> Thou who restorest the centuries,
> Thou who makest bloom the Spring,
> Thou who makest vibrate the musical chords.

> * * * * *

> Thou, splendor of my Spring, O Thou
> Sun reflected of millions of hearts.[13]

This hymn was published in Pravda in August 1936. In May 1935 the same official Party newspaper had published the following extraordinary effusion:

> He commands the sun of the enemies to set.
> He spoke, and the East for friends became a great glow

[13] Hallowell, *op. cit.*, p. 514.

Should he say that coal turn white,
It will be as Stalin wills. . . .
The master of the entire world—remember—is now Stalin.[14]

A much later composition by a leading Soviet poet shows development in style but hardly in subject matter.

I would have compared him to a white mountain—but
the mountain has a summit.
I would have compared him to the depths of the sea—but
the sea has a bottom.
I would have compared him to the shining moon—but
the moon shines at midnight, not at noon.
I would have compared him to the brilliant sun, but
the sun radiates at noon, not at midnight.[15]

These examples would appear to be characteristic, for leading critics affirm that the person of the Chief is the main topic and the real essence of poetry. "For a contemporary artist the conception of the Chief is the ideal incarnation of the philosophical conception of the people."[16]

REVIVAL OF IMPERIALISM

The second ominous development is the revival of Russian nationalism and imperialism. It is a truism now to point out that Stalin has done all the Czars remotely dreamed of and more by way of territorial expansion. Russia is in a position now to become in time, should things go well with the basic plan of ever greater industrialization and productivity, the richest and most favored nation in the world. There are observers who believe that nationalism is the real essence of Soviet Communism in its present phase. This was the point

[14] From *Communism and the Conscience of the West,* by Fulton J. Sheen, copyright 1948, used by special permission of the publishers, The Bobbs-Merrill Company, Inc., Indianapolis.
[15] Hallowell, *op. cit.,* p. 514.
[16] *Ibid.*

of view that dictated in part America's earlier Russian policy. It is a dangerous and unwarranted assumption. Nationalism is a dynamic force; it may become virtually a religion. It is an important factor in the new Russia. But it is insufficient to account for either Soviet psychology or behavior. Just as racialism was the really demonic element in German National Socialism, so Marxism with its Messianic exaltation of the proletariat and its *faith in history* remains the heart and nerve center of Soviet expansionism.

The third portent on the horizon of Communism and the world is the sign clearly there to read that the new system of faith and practice is up once more for world export. One knows that this is Kremlin policy—for in the Communist scheme nothing is left to chance or freedom—and suspects that some one has dreamed a new dream of a single world order, consisting of interlocked, interdependent Socialist Republics in every region of the globe, all Communist in bent and direction, all looking to the Kremlin as the fountainhead of truth and power, all marching together to the final goal of universal peace and classless brotherhood.

A NEW TOWER OF BABEL

It sounds fantastic—to us. But we have planners and dreamers a plenty taken up with one world. Would it be strange if the same obsession is strong in the minds of some of the Kremlin men, seeing especially that this was Marx's original idea? What a satisfaction it would be to fulfill after all the Marxist goal and confound the so much tougher than was expected, dialectically unaccommodating capitalist world! What a way to expiate the blood and torture and present continuing oppression of uncounted millions of human beings, workers not excepted! This last would, of course, be an unconscious motive and is an actually existent feeling only if Marxist theory is false and man is unable whatever his conditioning to escape a sense of guilt.

And they said [long, long ago, at the dawn of written history], Go to, let us build us a city, and a tower, whose top may reach to heaven.

This dream of universality and unity, this vision of a temple of man reaching far up into the skies and embracing heaven as well as earth, this imagination of human adequacy and essential divinity, is older than history as we are able to write it. Probably the materials utilized by the writer of the earliest stratum of the Old Testament were Babylonian and reflect the exultation felt by the architects of the first great civilization as they contemplated the wonder of their achievement. The capacity of man is limitless. He is as the gods. But catastrophe and disillusionment follow. The proud temple of man's building falls to the ground. Man's unity with his fellows is lost. Chaos and confusion follow. The dream of a building that would reach up into heaven is lost amid a buzzing Babel of tongues.

But the fault is not man's. It is not his incapacity or wickedness, but the jealousy of the gods, that has brought about the downfall of civilization. Even in the interpretation of the Biblical writer it is the Lord who, by creating a confusion of tongues and a consequent disruption of communication and coöperation, scatters men abroad "upon the face of all the earth." This, however, He does because He sees that nothing else will restrain the towering, infinite imagination of man.

Man has not forgotten his primitive dream. Now at the end of history, as the climax of the rise of science, the perfecting of technology, and the establishment of universal communication through all the world, he aspires to build again a tower that shall embrace earth and heaven, and make them forever one. This time there is nothing to restrain or confound him. The gods are gone, abiding only as faint ripples on the tablature of ancestral memory. The Semitic-Christian concept of one living and true God and its Indo-European counterpart of Absolute Being, have vanished nevermore to confuse the issues of life and divert man from the true labor of his own temple. As Marx put it, in a rhapsody of fervor and with an eloquence simulating cold and sober reason that shook the world:

Who has annihilated the dialectic of concepts, the war of the gods which the philosophers alone knew? Feuerbach. Who has put man in place of the old lumber, and in place of the infinite consciousness as well? Feuerbach.

Man makes religion; religion does not make man. . . .

Religion is the sigh of the oppressed creature, the feelings of a heartless world . . . the spirit of unspiritual conditions. It is the opium of the people. . . .

Thus it is the mission of history after the other-worldly truth has disappeared, to establish the truth of this world.

All mysteries which mislead theory to mysticism find their rational solution in human practice and in the comprehension of this practice.

Or, let us view the new tower of Babel through the eyes of an American missionary of Communism, William Z. Foster:

The proletarian revolution is the most profound of all revolutions in history. It initiates changes more rapid and far-reaching than any in the whole experience of mankind. The hundreds of millions of workers and peasants, striking off their age-old chains of slavery, will construct a society of liberty and prosperity and intelligence. Communism will inaugurate a new era for the human race. . . . [It] will bring about the immediate or eventual solution of many great social problems . . . war, religious superstition, prostitution, famine, pestilence, crime, poverty, alcoholism, unemployment, illiteracy, race and national chauvinism, the suppression of woman, and every form of slavery and exploitation of one class by another. . . .

For many generations the long list of utopians, the Platos, Mores, Fouriers, Owens, and Bellamys, have dreamed and planned ideal states of society. Their strong point was that they sensed mankind's capacity for a higher social life than the existing wild scramble. But their weak point, and this was decisive, was that they did not know what was the matter with society nor how to cure it. . . .

It has remained for the modern proletariat, under the brilliant leadership of Marx and Lenin, to find the revolutionary way to the higher social order, on the basis of the industrial and social conditions set up by capitalism. Marxians have been able to analyse capitalism scientifically, to work out a correct program and strategy of struggle . . . to master generally the laws of social development . . . and we may be sure that the revolution, in its upward course, will carry humanity to heights of happiness and achievement far beyond the dreams of even the most hopeful utopians.[17]

Conclusion

Such is the dream of the Communists. But the dream is a faith, an expectation, a power of patience, a certainty. It is a religion, a this-worldly universal salvation religion. This is the secret of the appeal of Communism in a tormented and empty, a hungry and thirsty, age. It offers a new world and it offers one world.

If the dream were all there is to Communism, it would perhaps be no cause for alarm. It is the embodiment of the dream in an intellectual system, in a *corpus* of faith and practice, in the power apparatus of the most highly developed police state in history, in an authoritarian socialist structure

[17] This quotation is from Foster's *Toward Soviet America* (1932). I owe the opportunity to consult this privately printed, extremely rare work to the kindness of Mrs. G. R. Baker.

of society embracing many nations but all in communion with Moscow, in the most massive, efficient, and highly trained missionary organization, with one possible exception, ever devised—it is all this that constitutes the menace and challenge of Communism.

In conclusion, as illustrative of the thesis of this book so far, that Communism can only be understood as a new religion in a new religious age and that for all its this-worldly modernity it parallels and parodies the development of other great religions, notably its rejected and hated mother, Christianity, we present a tabular comparison of the two contemporary religious rivals. Since working out this table and expounding it in various lectures, I find that Bishop Fulton J. Sheen has preceded me with this idea in his thoughtful work *Communism and the Conscience of the West* (pages 76, 77).[18] There are, however, several points of contrast as well as various likenesses in the two schemes.

A COMPARISON OF THE SYSTEMS OF CHRISTIANITY AND COMMUNISM

Christianity	*Communism*
The Living Creator God	Matter in Motion Dialetically Directed (=Dialectical Materialism)
The Trinity: Three Individuations in One Being: Three Persons of Revelation and Worship: F a t h e r, Christ, Spirit	Thesis, Antithesis, Synthesis: Capitalism, Proletariat Dictatorship, Communism: Marx the Lawgiver, Lenin the Incarnate Truth, Stalin the Guide and Comforter
The Chosen People or Israel of God	The Proletariat, Destined to Inherit the Earth

[18] Sheen, *op. cit.*

Christianity	*Communism*
Evil—which is Sin and Death	Private Property—Source of All Social Ills
Redemption by the Cross and Passion of Christ	Revolution by the Torment and Blood of the Proletariat
The Church: Organ of Truth, Source of Sanctification, Mediator of Redemption	The Party:[19] Organ of Action, Enlightenment, Discipline for the Proletariat
The Scriptures: Old and New Testaments	Marxism-Leninism: Writings of Marx and Words and Deeds of Lenin
Internal Witness of the Holy Spirit (Protestantism) or In-fallible Interpreter (the Pope)	The Will and Word of Stalin
Love and Sacrifice: The Law of the Kingdom of Heaven	Force and Violent Class Struggle: The Law of Progress toward the Classless Society
The Last Judgment: Separation of Sheep and Goats, Saints and Sinners	The Violent Overthrow of Capitalists and Enthronement of the Workers
The Millennium: Christ's Reign in a Transformed Heaven and Earth	The Withering Away of the State in a Classless Brotherhood
Sacrament of the Real Presence	The Ceaseless Exposure of the Perpetually Renewed Body of Lenin—both on State Occasions and for All the People

[19] In Munich in 1939 when I asked two young Nazis, graduates of one of the "Fuehrer Schools" or Ordensburgen, what would take the place of the Church in history, they replied unhesitatingly: "The Party." Hitler's tutor in the concept of the Party was, of course, Lenin.

II

The Background of Communism

There be gods many, and lords many.
—*I Corinthians 8:5.*

THE THESIS of this chapter and of the present work as a whole is that we are living in a new historical period. The dominant motives are not, as in the past six hundred years, reason and scientific knowledge. Instead they are religious, mystical, and personal.

The great aim of man in the new age is not to win mastery by knowledge but to find personal well-being through union with forces and powers greater than himself. This is the meaning of *religious* in its broadest sense. Religion, in contrast to science and philosophy, describes the urge of man to reach out beyond himself and his own powers and faculties and to seek power and peace through alliance with that which is other than and greater than himself. This *other* is usually thought of as God or a god. But it may mean a superhuman earthly power such as a State, an absolute ruler, or some natural reality like sex or race.

OLDER MEANING OF "RELIGION"

In past ages the term "religion" was used in this neutral, general sense, to cover many kinds and degrees of a specific activity. We must return to the older usage, for the time is past when we can view all religious manifestations as essentially one and as more or less true. Instead of an evolutionary understanding of religion as fondly worked out by the high priests of progress in the nineteenth century, we are forced by stubborn facts to speak of false and true religion.

This was in St. Paul's mind when about 55 A.D. he was writing the small church he had founded in the wealthy, licentious seaport city of Corinth. The point he is concerned with is a problem of morals and psychology—eating meat that has been previously sacrificed to idols in some pagan temple. Why not! he exclaims. What is an idol? Nothing at all. There is no God but one. Then he thinks of all the temples, all the cults, all the sacrifices, all the religions of men. "For although there may be so-called gods in heaven or on earth—as indeed there are many 'gods' and many 'lords'—yet for us there is one God, the Father, from whom are all things and for whom we exist, and one Lord Jesus Christ, through whom are all things and through whom we exist."[1]

In these words we have as a backdrop for a great statement of the faith of Christianity building upon Judaism, a description of the religious situation in the Graeco-Roman world. "There be gods many, and lords many." It was a time of turning to religion and of seeking that which religion alone offers, namely, strength for weakness, renewal of depleted spiritual energy, through union with something greater and better than oneself.

THE ERA BEFORE CHRIST

When Christ was born, it was almost six centuries since Thales of Miletus, a commercial city of the Greeks in Southern Asia Minor, had turned away from the explanations of believers in the gods and had asserted that everything in

[1] I Corinthians 8:5, RSV.

nature went back to one primal element, water. The earth, he said, rests on water, and out of it come all other substances. This was the birth of science and of Western philosophy, and the two have continued in close if not always easy relationship down to the present day.

Another philosopher of the same school, Anaximander, held that the original substance could not be water, earth, air, or fire. If it were any one of these or any known element, he said, it would conquer the others. Therefore the primal substance is something that is unknown, but it is infinite, eternal, and ageless; and "it encompasses all the worlds."

Still other thinkers said that everything comes from some other known but primal element, as air or fire. The fire-hypothesis, popularized by the brilliant intellect of Heraclitus, won the greatest favor, and was for centuries the foundation of the cosmology of the Stoics. All things begin and end, say the Stoics, in fire. But it is a peculiar kind of fire. It is instinct with "logos," logic, reason, law, a Divine principle, God.

The early, somewhat simple-minded Greek philosophers were followed by a series of intellects as brilliant and fertile as the world has seen. The classical succession reaches its climax and zenith in Plato and Aristotle. Of the first, a very great modern, the late Professor Alfred North Whitehead of Trinity, Cambridge, and Harvard, has said:

> The most satisfactory general characterization that can be given of European philosophy is, that it is a series of footnotes to Plato.

Aristotle has been called the world's first professor. It was he who set out to do two things. One was to infuse common sense into the system of his master Plato. The second was to approach with the first principles thus gained all fields of human endeavor and learning and to map out the whole world of knowledge. This monumental enterprise was carried out so thoroughly and so well that for nearly two thousand years the world of science and learning rested solidly on the shoulders of the Atlas of the intellect, Aristotle.

The inward aim of knowledge is always mastery. It reveals the human spirit in an active, athletic role. The key-phrase by which we identify and describe this side of man is reason. The classical Greek period, lasting from roughly 585 B.C. to 35 B.C. is an age of reason. Only one other period in history is comparable to it—the age of which we unwitting have seen the demise: the Age of Science, which began somewhere around 1350 A.D. and which ended with the coming of the First World War in 1914.

RELIGION AND FAITH

Religion has as its inward motive and form, not mastery but surrender. It is much closer to love than to knowledge. Indeed it may be that in its essence it is another name for love. It reveals the human spirit in a passive, receptive role. It works not by reason, though reason is in no way necessarily excluded from being a large part even of the religious life—but by faith. For the religious man, faith is the very form of existence. The key-word of the entire Bible is faith, just as the master-phrase of the Greek tradition is "logos" or reason. In a Letter written around 90 A.D. the second creative thinker produced by the Christian Church said:

Now faith is the assurance of things hoped for, the conviction of things not seen. For by it the men of old received divine approval.[2]

This wonderful definition of faith applies not merely to the religion of the Bible. It applies to all religion. It is the

[2] Hebrews 11:1, 2, RSV. (It is certain that this Epistle is not written by Paul the Apostle, as any reader of the Epistle even in English can determine for himself.)

key to the psychology of man as a religious animal through-out his history and not least today in the heart and center of a prodigious industrial and technical world-economy. There are not a few signs that we are now in the midst of a great shift in the tide of human becoming, and that the shift is from reason to faith, from science to religion, from the mastery of self-assertion and self-confidence to the surrender of self in union with superhuman being and power.

THE ANCIENT MYSTERY RELIGIONS

Once before in the clear light of history a development of this kind occurred. It coincided with the decline of Greece and the transformation of the Republic of Rome into the Roman Empire. Along with fundamental political and economic movements there was the most marked religious ferment. Out of the East, ancient cradle of religions, there was a constant procession Westward of new faiths. The celebrated Greek Mysteries—the Eleusinian, the Dionysiac, the Orphic—were revived in fresh forms and under novel Asiatic and Egyptian names. These mystic rites had flourished long before the birth of philosophy. In the time of Socrates and Plato, at the height of the glory of Athens, they were still a notable feature of the common life of the City.

With the conquests of the great Alexander and the establishment after him of the Greek Kingdoms, the Mysteries lost their appeal and became stagnant. Perhaps because of the export far and wide of the concepts and mentality of the philosophers, religion in both Greece and Asia witnessed its low-water mark. But as the world rolled on and the lamp of reason flickered somewhat and the multitudes found no satisfaction in the gospel of Stoic self-reliance and the rigorous control of passion by reason, a rash of new and revived mystery religions arose and with unprecedented power spread throughout the whole Graeco-Roman world. The city of Rome, to which increasingly all roads led, seems to have been their goal and often became their center and focal point.

Among the most popular of the new faiths were the cult of Cybele, the Great Mother, and Abbis, which came from Asia Minor; the Phoenician or Syrian cult of Astarte and Adonis (or Baal), going back to the worship against which the prophet Elijah contended; and the cult of Isis and Osiris (or Serapis) imported from Egypt. Somewhat later, in the second century A.D., the Persian religion of Mithra, the sun-god, made rapid headway in the Empire and was in special favor with the Roman Legions. Another religion which was beginning to spread widely at the beginning of the Christian Era was Gnosticism. The name comes from the Greek word *gnosis* or knowledge and its use was not unlike that of science from *scientia* or knowledge in Christian Science. This very powerful spiritual movement was a combination of mystery religion and speculative philosophy. In addition to offering salvation from a "fallen" material world, it undertook to explain in terms of a fanciful and baroque drama of the heavenly powers how evil came about and why the unfortunate event of creation ever occurred at all. Gnosticism was the first adversary of Christianity and probably the most formidable in its long history.

In all these religions the salvation interest is predominant. They offer the individual enlargement of life, consolation of mind, and assurance of victory over death and entrance into an immortal sphere. An element common to them is a divine saviour, a god or lord who has passed through the experience of dying and rising again and who as lord of a particular cult offers to the believing initiate union with himself in this experience. The figure of the suffering deity is commonly vague and crudely conceived; it is always bound up with other interests and deities appropriate to them. Nevertheless, it is most arresting and significant that the Christ had many forerunners among the Gentiles and that the figure of a Redeemer was already present under various forms when Christianity came upon the scene.

WHY CHRISTIANITY WON OUT

The religion destined to win out over all rivals and to command the future, began as a movement within Judaism. That faith, it is worth noting, had already won the attention of many earnest souls and seems to have attracted especially high-born women in court circles at Rome. Christianity does not seem to have had much in common with the religions of the Gentiles during the life-time of Jesus or in the early presentation of its message or in a large and important section of the Church down to the end of the first century. The proof of this is the first three or "Synoptic" Gospels, the Acts, and Epistles like Hebrews and James. Here the affinities are with the mother-religion of Israel, although it cannot be stated too strongly that there is no record of any Christianity without Jesus Christ being personally and dynamically at its center.

Yet beyond any doubt the new religion made its way in the Gentile world and met the needs of plain men and women not because of its likenesses to Judaism but rather because of its affinities with the Mysteries. *If these latter had not existed, Christianity would not have become a universal religion and conquered the Roman Empire*. It was the work of the converted Rabbi, Saul of Tarsus, renamed Paul, to see and bring into clear focus the fulfillment in Christ of the thirst for a dying god and a risen lord. St. Paul's contribution here, which is so momentous, was in the realm of interpretation, of insight, of personal love of Christ, of mystical self-identification with the death and resurrection of the Lord. Paul claimed as a discovery no new facts but specifically rested his Gospel on the facts received from Peter and the other Apostles. Yet the Christianity of St. Paul for all its solid Jewishness of background and for all its foursquare agreement factually with common Christian tradition is a mystery religion of salvation. It appealed to people for the same reasons as the current Mysteries though at an infinitely higher level.

Pauline Christianity is continued in the writings of the third great Christian thinker, St. John. The Gospel produced by this great lover as well as thinker is something utterly unique. It is the supreme work of genius in Christian and religious history. In it a genuine special tradition of times and events is incorporated, supplementing and correcting the traditions of the Synoptists, Mark, Matthew, and Luke. But the real interest of the author is not in history and biography as these are understood by the modern mind. His interest is in the spiritual Christ—in the ultimate being and meaning of the one who came to earth, lived, died, and rose to immortality. The Christ of St. John is the Christ of faith unveiled; He is in many respects a contrast to the Synoptic Christ but the contrast is incidental to enlargement of spiritual vision. In between the two is the insight and the love of St. Paul. The Christ of St. John in consequence is, in a famous phrase from a renowned scholar, a speaking, acting Pauline Christ. He is the Lord of the Church around 100 A.D. presented and portrayed ideally, without the sense of time, development, and necessary consistency which are the marks of our kind of historical research. The miracle

of this Gospel is that the result is not an incredible mythological figure but a being who is personal, real, and appealing in the highest sense. The drama of divine-human love
which is the essence of the Christ and of His religion is in
this Gospel heightened and glorified. The message of St.
John is that love is sacrifice, and that God being love could
not do other than give Himself in and as Christ. The meaning also of being in Christ as an initiate and believer is to
love God and the brethren. In the sacraments of Baptism
and the Supper of the Lord or Holy Communion, each
rite symbolizing the death and resurrection of the Lord, the
believer is joined to Christ, receives His Spirit, participates
in His dramatic, tragic, triumphant, saving experience, and
partakes of deathless life. Christianity, in other words, is
identification with Christ.

It is thus that the Christian religion confronted and conquered the world in the first centuries of this era. This age
was one of the most religious of which we have any record.
In it men reached out thirstily for God, fulfilling the words
of the Hebrew song writer:

> As the hart panteth after the water brooks,
> so panteth my soul after thee, O God.[3]

They did so because they had a deep sense of their insuffi-
ciency and need. They did so because they found life in
isolation too much for them and were compelled to face
the overwhelming reality of "a failure of nerve."[4] Christianity
won out in the fiercest religious struggle because it was
foremost in satisfying the desire, healing the nerve, and
renewing the being of man.

[3] Psalm 42:1.
[4] A phrase borrowed by Sir Gilbert Murray from Prof. J. B. Bury.

The West in a New Religious Phase

What of our age? What of the new period that began sometime in the present century and is already manifestly novel and different in its basic psychology? Beyond question it is more like the first decades and centuries of the Christian Era than any previous time before or since Christ. It is a period too of "gods many, and lords many." It is a period of "failure of nerve" or in our lingo, insecurity. Men are turning from science and from reason as sufficient of itself just as they did then. Also they are turning from individual self-reliance and social optimism just as in the earlier time Stoicism, the ideology of Roman republicanism and of the vital early stages of imperial expansion, lost its hold and failed utterly to satisfy the heart and soul.

There are many signs that the Western world has entered a new religious phase—not wholly different from that of the first Christian centuries. When we say the West we really mean the entire world, for the world is now one in respect of communication and the tide is now in full flood from West to East, reversing the condition of ancient man. Then it was a matter of the undermining and suffocation of the Roman spirit: "the West expires in the embrace of the East." Today it is the East which is in danger of complete alteration. Ideas, influences, standards, world-views, religious movements, pour out of the West and mold anew the ancient and religious East. Communism, which originated in the British Museum, London, in the mind of an exiled German Jew, is simply the latest and most phenomenal example. From a mind and a voluminous, abstruse book to the garrets and parlors of the Socialists of Europe; from failure and disillusionment in Europe to victory in Russia by the instrumentality of a sealed railway carriage and the blindness of the German High Command; from Russia to China and one quarter of the earth's people!

Science, technology, the mastery of matter, the improvement of living standards—these are the distinctive achievements of the West in Eastern eyes and the reason for reversal of spiritual traffic between the two main sectors of the planet. They will remain dominant factors in the life of man—unless total war comes and civilization is engulfed in unrelieved catastrophe. Yet his valuation of technical rationality and his confidence in the sufficiency of his own powers and values have altered. Western man is not what he was. He is in a chastened and frightened mood. He is reaching out to something beyond himself and greater than himself. His psychology is increasingly religious. His world exhibits the return of "gods many, and lords many."

Signs and Evidences: Seven Fields of Fact

What are the signs and evidences that we are in a new religious age? They are so numerous that a simple serial listing would be tedious. We shall, therefore, organize them by reference to basic fields of fact in our world and shall then attempt to survey briefly these magnetic fields, as it were, of influence and radiating power. It must of course be remembered that life is something highly concrete and is always a unity of many forces. Classification is necessarily abstract and artificial. It is like dissection in the medical classroom. The unity of the concrete whole or wholes is lost, but there is no other way to study the various parts that together make up any total reality.

Let us, therefore, undertake, at least as a start, the vivisection of our age. If we are at all successful, other more skillful physicians of the spirit and of society may be stimulated to carry on a most necessary task.

There are, at least, seven fields of fact which seem to be significant indicators of what is happening to modern man. They are submitted as evidence of a far-reaching thesis, namely, that a period prevailingly dominated by the sentiment of rationality has ended, and has been succeeded by one of all-pervading religiousness. These fields of fact are:

1. Religious Revival.
2. The Thrust toward the Sensate and the Sensual.
3. Insecurity—a Collective Neurosis.
4. The New Demons.
5. Psychiatry—a New Priesthood.
6. Existentialism: or Subjectivity in Rebound.
7. The Rise of a New World Religion.

(1) Religious Revival

It is now possible to say certainly that America as a whole is experiencing a religious revival. For long I have been unsure personally as to the broad trends in this area and have suspended judgment. The evidence is now conclusive that a major quickening of the religious impulse is under way and is manifest in diverse ways.

First, there are more Church members today proportionately as well as actually than ever before in the history of the United States. The current figure is 85,705,280 or 55.9 per cent of the Nation's 153,085,000 people. In 1900 the per cent figure was 34.7. The Protestant total of 50,083,868 does not include for the most part baptized children or younger Sunday School pupils. If these were included, as they are in the case of Episcopalians (included in the Protestant figure) and the Roman Catholics, the total would be swelled by at least twenty-five, possibly by as much as thirty-five, per cent. In addition, there are several hundred small sects not included in the data of the *Christian Herald* Survey, from which the figures cited above are taken. And it seems reasonable to suppose that in this roomy land with its very high rate of moving about from place to place, there are several million lapsed and discarded Church members. This reflection is of value at least as an offset to "padded" lists or the retention on the rolls of very nominal members. It is supported by what happens in all Christian Churches on Easter and in not a few at Christmas Eve Midnight and on Palm Sunday.

We are instinctively suspicious of statistics. The wag who declared that there are three kinds of lies—lies, damn lies, and statistics—reflected the prejudice of most of us. Yet an impartial observer is bound to concede the extraordinary impressiveness of the Church statistics which roll out year by year.

Second, the fringe sects and more emotional and folkish denominations are showing a phenomenal increase, both in the birth of new organized cults and in making new converts. The fastest growing bodies in America today appear to be the Church of God in Christ and the Assemblies of God. Of the old-line Protestant bodies the Southern Baptists are out-stripping all rivals in speed of increase. There is evidence that the industrial millions in America's "heart-land" of the Middle West are taking to religion in earnest, influenced by the vacuum of assembly-line existence, the contagion of stepped-up insecurity, and the example of neighbors from the South who have brought "religion" with them. Here is one of the supreme opportunities as well as perils of contemporary America.

Third, there is the revival of revivalism. The writer was brought up near an edge of the Bible Belt but well within it. He may claim to be an expert, in virtue of actual experience, on the type of revivalism of which Billy Sunday became the leading symbol. By an accident of friendship it happened, also, that he was the first Episcopal rector in the United States to invite the Rev. Bryan Green, England's twentieth century John Wesley, to conduct a mission. At this time Green stated, having just completed a six months tour principally of schools, colleges, and universities in the American hinterland, that never in his experience had he seen such hunger of soul as among these young people. Five years later Bishops were vying with one another to claim his services.

Green is now a national institution, with engagements years ahead, as well as a traveler throughout the British Commonwealth of Nations. Meanwhile local products have advanced to national celebrity. As this book is coming off the press Billy Graham, who may prove a new Whitefield, will be holding a mammoth revival, sponsored by at least one Senator of the United States, within the shadow of the Capitol Dome in Washington. Other figures are coming to the fore, such as Oral Roberts and Gayle Jackson, the first a faith-healer as well as an evangelist. An American reporter, sent out to scout and report on these men, writes that "this summer revivals are firing the body of American Protestantism with a heat it hasn't felt in a hundred years."

It is logical to suppose that what we have seen thus far is a mild portent of what is to come, as heat lightning often presages a violent and thunderous electrical storm. The psychological tinder of an immense spiritual conflagration is present. A strong spark may at any time ignite it.

Fourth, there is a widespread turning to authority in

religion. Dean Inge remarked twenty-five years back that the only two bodies which seemed to be gaining converts were religions of authority—Roman Catholicism and Christian Science. This trend continues and on a more or less international scale. It is reported by non-Roman Catholic observers that the influence of this body in devastated and disillusioned Germany is very great and extends to Evangelicals and "Humanists." It is notable that the Protestant bodies cited above and aggressive missionary sects like the Mormons and Adventists are strongly authoritarian in temper, in propaganda, and in appeal. Finally and in passing, it should not be overlooked that the three big totalitarian movements of our generation, Communism, Fascism, and National Socialism, came as political religions and denoted a violent pendulum swing from freedom and self-reliance to authority and submission. Mussolini, the most European of the dictators, once remarked that humanity was going through a passive and feminine phase.

Fifth, at the very moment of the greatest advances of scientific and technical reason there is an outbreak of the most extreme credulity. The masses believe as much as ever, and probably intellectuals do, too. "He who believes nothing, can be made to believe anything." When religion becomes too rationalized, superstition crops out in unexpected places. It is as if man's appetite to believe must somehow be satisfied. Was it not William Blake who wrote:

Man must and will have some religion: and if he has not the religion of Jesus, he will have the religion of Satan and will erect the Synagogue of Satan, calling the Prince of this world, God, and destroying all who do not worship Satan under the name of God.

At any rate, and without presuming to apply to any of them the label of Satanic, we see all round us literate middle class people turning to astrology, spiritualism, "metaphysics," theosophy, reincarnation, "science," unity, Bahai, spiritual healing, the gospel according to Emmet Fox or Frank Buchman, the Great I Am, the Great White Brotherhood (which, gentle reader, for your information is "apparently an organized coterie of Spirit-Intelligences who have made it their business to influence earth-folk for their own spiritual benefit and well-being"), and so on and so on.

There is literally no belief that one cannot encounter in a more or less run-of-the-mill professional life. A retired Episcopal clergyman, of pronouncedly liberal views, claims to have had converse with the spirit of the late Bishop Freeman at a spiritualist seance and to have heard from him a soulful homily. Not many months back I met a French Count with a nine hundred years name and a tall, aristocratic figure. When I raised the question of the future of politics in France, I learned that the secret was in the stars and that all depended upon the as yet imperfectly disclosed exertions of heavenly powers. A lady on her death bed declined the Sacrament and professed disbelief in Sin. She believed in "metaphysics" but admired extravagantly three eminent clergymen of the Episcopal Church. One day she said: "You know, it finally came to me who the Magi *are*." Before I could reveal that I had entirely failed to follow her train of thought, she went on: "They are Doctor X., Dean Y., and Bishop Z."

That is what the Church history books, speaking of the second and third centuries, call Syncretism.

Sixth, there is in our troubled time a quiet but growing revival of mysticism and a return to the practice of prayer. There is often the associated idea of spiritual cells or informal small communities of seekers after God. The two groups which are doing most to foster this trend are, in the United States, the Quakers, under the leadership of Douglas Steere and Elton Trueblood, and the Neo-Vedantists, under the leadership of Gerald Heard and Aldous Huxley. Heard is not only a mystic and a devotee to an extent that recalls the first Christian monks; he is also a versatile if rather far-ranging scientist and a brilliant constructive theologian. The French scientist Alexis Carrel also made a profound impression in this connection by his book *Man the Unknown* and popular articles on prayer.

In Great Britain there is the Iona Community under the sponsorship of the Presbyterian Church of Scotland and there is the quite considerable and ever growing influence of the religious communities of the Church of England. One has the impression in these Churches of a deeper piety and a more real mystical life than anything we know in American Protestantism. On the other hand, the gulf between Church devotion and the life of the people seems in the older countries to be very wide and to be growing wider. Over here the Churches are to an extraordinary degree a popular enterprise. It may be, however, that the most important thing happening today is the endeavor to leave aside the world of the senses and the furniture of the conscious mind and to descend into the neglected interior of our being, there to make contact with the Infinite Ground of all.

This brings us directly to another salient characteristic of our age.

(2) THE THRUST TO THE SENSATE AND THE SENSUAL

"Sensate" is the eminent Harvard sociologist, Professor Sorokin's word for a culture preoccupied with reality as known through the five senses. "Only what we see, hear, smell, touch, and otherwise perceive through our sense-organs is real and has value." Sensate culture is in contrast to "ideational" culture—an order of life and thought based on "the principle of a supersensory and superrational God as the only true reality and value." Western mediaeval culture was ideational, as was that of Brahmanic India, Buddhism, Taoism, and Greece prior to 500 B.C. In between, Sorokin posits an "idealistic" culture or a blending into a unity of the sensory and supersensory principles with an emphasis upon reason. This culture he appears to regard as little more than a transitional phase between the more basic ideational and sensate patterns.

Sorokin holds that we stand at the present moment in the twilight of a brilliant Sensate day which has lasted six hundred years. The present crisis denotes that we are in between the Sensate Era of yesterday and a coming creative Ideational culture.[5] Sorokin holds that the advent of the latter is certain, and is as optimistic in ultimate outlook as Oswald Spengler is pessimistic.

Sorokin's view of past, present, and future is closely related to the analysis and thesis of this chapter. I am inclined to think that he has things too neatly arranged and catalogued and that he is too naive in his balancing of pessimism and optimism. Perhaps reality is wilder and more unpredictable than any scheme of logic can encompass. This seems to follow from the fact of freedom and of history as the field in which freedom is operative as the basic form of existence. It is from this angle that totalitarianism represents so grave a threat and challenge, and likewise that the possibilities of

[5] See his *The Crisis of Our Age* (New York, E. P. Dutton and Company) and other works.

response on the part of free men and democratic institutions are unlimited.

There can be no question that ours is a sensate culture in Sorokin's sense. The thrust toward the sensate remains very powerful and is abetted by modern communications and an omnipresent and almost omnipotent commercialism. The final phase of sensate development seems to be absorption and obsession by the sexual.

We are far advanced in this phase. American culture is sex-drenched to a degree without precedent in history. This is not because we are especially sensual as a people. We are probably far less so than the Germans, the Russians, or the French. But we are very vulnerable psychologically because we are still half-Puritan and on our other side we are romantic rather than realistic. American motion pictures illustrate most neatly both sides of this analysis: our sensual suggestibility and our romanticism.

One thinks by contrast of France. There sensuality is at once an art and an assumption. This being a settled matter, the French are able to get on with other business. They seem singularly free from sex-obsession and their simplicity in the use of leisure, in eating and drinking, in family life, in the acceptance by both sexes that men are men and women are women, is an achievement of the order of genius.

The other reason for the blatancy and constancy of American exposure to sensual stimulus is, again, the place of advertising and of business competition in the national life. The aim of salesmanship is to gain attention and induce conviction. An unwritten axiom of advertising is: Sex-appeal, or the desire to have it, never fails.

A delicious satire on the state of things to which we have thus attained is the improvement over the movies posited by

Aldous Huxley in the Utopia which is the central theme of his novel of two decades ago, *Brave New World*. One enters an Entertainment Palace, as I recall it, in that Paradise of social engineering and psychological conditioning directed from the top, and instead of the movies there are the feelies. No longer is one limited to seeing and imagination. In front of each row of seats is a metal rail. One puts out a hand and takes hold of it, then feels directly the sensations of love.

Meanwhile things do not stand still. One in every four marriages ends in divorce. Happiness in love and marriage is increasingly rare, and is difficult both to attain and retain. Sexual irregularity and license as attested by Kinsey's and other reports, are endemic in proportion. Above all, the sins of the fathers are visited on the children, who grow up unstable, undisciplined, and precociously immature in emotional and love experience. Insecurity, already a menacing disease of the soul, is multiplied beyond estimation.

(3) INSECURITY—A COLLECTIVE NEUROSIS

The ancient world, we are told, experienced a general failure of nerve. J. B. Bury suggested this diagnosis when Gilbert Murray called the change observable between Plato and, four hundred years later, the Neo-Platonists a rise of asceticism, or mysticism, or religious passion.[6] Bury felt that it was not a rise but a fall or failure. The reconciliation of these two seemingly opposed accounts is given by our thesis that religious need follows the failure of individual self-reliance.

We, too, know what failure of nerve is. It is writ large in recent history. It has gripped whole peoples. It is an under-

[6] Murray, Preface to *Five Stages of Greek Religion* (London: Watts & Co., Ltd.).

lying, universal aspect of our age of crisis, a crisis that, above all, is centered in man's outlook on himself and his world.

We do not speak as a rule of failure of nerve. We speak of insecurity. This phrase, which like "maturity" is almost an ultimate category of psychology but is not easy to define, describes very well the temperature, or perhaps a better figure would be the barometric existence-pressure, of our time and culture.

What is the strongest drive in America today—at an hour of frightful peril but also of stirring challenge and infinite opportunity? It is the drive for security, for safety, for insurance against loss and trouble. It is expressed in many forms and at many points. Very dominating is the drive of economic security. This involves politics and requires a conception of the nature and role of the state that is a reversal of the classical concept of negative, minimal government enunciated by Jefferson and other founding fathers. The security drive is paramount, also, or is liable to be in the choice of vocation. It tends to be an obsession in love-relationships, beginning with very young teen-agers. It is formative in the contemporary approach to religion. What is wanted of the Church, by and large, is not challenge, not direction in prayer, morals, or social issues, but comfort, assurance, clear definiteness in what is to be believed, the impartation of certainty about God and about human destiny here and hereafter. The old word for this is salvation, which means literally safety and might be defined as ultimate security. At this point we can see the relation between the mounting neurotic insecurity of our time and religion.

The final insecurity is cosmic insecurity. It is the sense of irremediable isolation and homelessness. It is the persuasion that man is an alien and a stranger, not only as he voyages through time, but irrevocably, ultimately, and absolutely. Outside the small worlds which he has made, beyond the minute patterns of order and meaning here and there which are called civilizations and which he has created, there is nothing save only the dark and everlasting night.

> But now I only hear
> Its melancholy, long, withdrawing roar,
> Retreating, to the breath
> Of the night wind, down the vast edges drear
> And naked shingles of the world.
> Ah, love, let us be true
> To one another! for the world, which seems
> To lie before us like a land of dreams,
> So various, so beautiful, so new,
> Hath really neither joy, nor love, nor light,
> Nor certitude, nor peace, nor help for pain;
> And we are here as on a darkling plain
> Swept with confused alarms of struggle and flight
> Where ignorant armies clash by night.

These lines, written at the high-water mark of the Victorian and nineteenth century achievement by a peerless master of words, and meant probably by Arnold as the expression simply of a mood, are actually an acute prophecy. They indicate that a new anguish awaits the human spirit. They foretell that the long nightmare of a fate implacable and impersonal, from which Christ once freed man, enabling him to recover his energies and powers, is about to return.

It has returned, unnerving and undoing man once more. It is the real explanation of the underlying neurosis of present mankind. It is the reason why our era is "the Age of Anxiety." In his poem on this theme W. H. Auden dissects the situation and with the grim ruthlessness now in favor among poets and artists tells us what has happened.

> Storm invades
> The Euclidean calm. The clouds explode.
> The scene dissolves, is succeeded by
> A grinning gap, a growth of nothing
> Pervaded by vagueness.
>   * * *
>
> Sob, heavy world,
> Sob as you spin
> Mantled in mist, remote from the happy.
>   * * *
>
> Away the cylinder seal,
> The didactic digit and the dreaded voice
> Which impose peace on the pullulating
> Primordial mess. Mourn for him now,
> Our lost dad,
> Our colossal father.[7]

(4) THE NEW DEMONS

The earliest description perhaps that we have of the Christian mission is that it was an assault upon the forces of evil understood in terms of demons or demonic powers. St. Mark's trenchant summary of the work of Jesus is that "he went throughout all Galilee, preaching in their synagogues and casting out demons."[8]

The subject of the preaching was God and the Divine Kingdom now breaking in upon the life of the world. "Jesus came into Galilee, preaching the gospel of God, and saying, The time is fulfilled, and the kingdom of God is at hand; repent [or be transformed in your mind], and believe in the gospel."[9] But the coming of the Kingdom was not only in word; it was also in power. This meant assault upon the

[7] W. H. Auden, *The Age of Anxiety* (New York, Random House, 1947). Used by permission.
[8] St. Mark 1:39, RSV.
[9] St. Mark 1:14, RSV.

fallen spirits of the upper air or demons, who ranged abroad over the earth and brought man all manner of ill, sometimes even possessing his body and living as it were on top of his spirit. People thus possessed were called demoniacs.

To us this language and the background of thought behind it are strange, and I for one remain a modern in suspecting that we shall not simply return to the thought-forms of ancient demonology. It is important, however, to remember that this mode of conceiving and explaining the reality of evil was universal in the world at that time. It was the same in Ephesus, in Athens, in Rome, as in Palestine. When St. Paul wrote the Ephesian Christians (or it may be that it was a disciple of Paul and the editor of the first collection of his letters, accompanying them with a kind of covering Encyclical), he stated in classic terms the outlook of ancient man:

> For we are not contending against flesh and blood, but against the principalities, against the powers, against the world rulers of this present darkness, against the spiritual hosts of wickedness in the heavenly places. Therefore take the whole armor of God. . . .[10]

The writer of these words was not dealing with an immediate emergency or a concrete medical problem. His aim was to give a general picture of the cosmic situation, as it bore on the existence of every Christian and every man. The odd thing is that his description is as modern today as when he wrote it. It portrays the present situation, including the existence of each of us. It depicts nations, races, classes, individuals and groups in power. I can think of no other passage, unless it be St. Matthew's acount of Christ's temptation in the Wilderness, that so illuminates what has happened in our reactionary, "possessed," evil time.

[10] Ephesians 6:12, 13, RSV

An illustration from personal experience will clarify the point better than several pages of abstract analysis. In late August, 1939, I was in Switzerland attending a small Ecumenical Conference which was torpedoed—along with so much more than conferences—by the dramatic sudden news, heard by some one listening to a B. B. C. broadcast, of the Russo-German Pact. Several members of the Conference left at once. I, with some others, lingered till the next day to take a morning train to Paris. One of the latter group was a little German of Semitic extraction but Lutheran faith who had been compelled to emigrate and settle in Switzerland. He had won an Iron Cross in World War I and was deeply German at heart, full of sentiment about the past and of self-pity respecting the present. We talked till late into the night, and he stated simply and without any hedging that it would be war. I had just been traveling in Germany and had been impressed by the extraordinary prosperity evident on all sides, by the security and confidence enjoyed by most of the people, and by Hitler's interest in the arts, in housing, in public buildings, and in roads. So I argued that he wanted peace to preserve and continue his great internal program. My little friend was unimpressed. Yes, he said, in his human heart Hitler wants peace. But it will be war. *Die Daemonen ihn haben* (The demons have got him).

This naive sentimental German exile had a keener insight than I. His intuition schooled in the New Testament was more accurate than my analogical reasoning based on the terms and reactions of a normal human being. How right he was about Hitler! That brilliant madman was in the grip of powers stronger than himself. It was not a question of flesh and blood, but of principalities and powers.

Then there is the case of one Josef Stalin, who in 1944-

1945 pulled off the greatest game of bluff and steal in many a century—perhaps in all time. He convinced Franklin Delano Roosevelt and Winston Churchill that he was a changed character, an essentially genial and good human being, and first-rate democratic timber. It was a dreadful miscalculation, yet entirely natural. Without doubt Stalin is a human being, capable of being nice, playful, and generous. But there is so much more to it. He too is in the grip— explain, describe it as we will—of trans-human, demonic, inexorable forces. Roosevelt and Churchill and our world would have fared so much better if they had happened to believe in the New Testament doctrine of demons.

This of course was impossible. The reason is that Western man had long before ceased to believe in evil. He became persuaded that all things, including men and nations and societies, are rational and are moving toward perfection. He let down all barriers and forgot the safeguards and checks within and without devised and practiced by his ancestors for a hundred generations. The result was not tranquility, was not persisting progress ever onward and always upward. The result was an outreach and onrush of new demons, fresh and strong from resting a couple of aeons, well ready to undertake the arduous task of diverting mankind from the straight path of ceaseless advance and swinging it on to a historical roller-coaster on a course planetary in range. We are all riding now on this monster, whether we like it or not, whether we have yet waked up to the fact or not. This language is mythological, as much so as that of Jesus Christ in the days of His flesh over nineteen hundred years ago.

When the unclean spirit is gone out of a man, he walketh through dry places, seeking rest; and finding none, he saith, I will return unto my house whence I came out. And when he cometh, he findeth it swept and garnished. Then goeth he, and taketh to him seven other spirits more wicked than himself; and they enter in, and dwell there: and the last state of that man is worse than the first.[11]

The final explanation we shall never know—in this order. There is a "mystery of iniquity" which is beyond our understanding but not our experience. This much we can perhaps say. A person or a group becomes demonic when it acts as if something relative and finite is the absolute and all. To be demonic is to treat as of unconditional validity and force that which is conditional and partial. The structures of created being, individual, social, and historical, are such as to give ready lodgment to the demonic. Once deeply entrenched, the demonic spirit feeds more and more on itself, banishes reason, temperance, and justice, and acts as if the creature is Creator, the man or nation or race or culture not itself but Almighty God. When this happens to a sufficient degree, we may say that we are dealing no longer with the merely demonic, but with the Satanic, with Antichrist. This, however, is a perilous judgment for a mortal, and but for Jesus Christ would be impossible. It was perhaps for this reason that He came into our world of sin, Satan, and death.

(5) Psychiatry—A New Priesthood

The characteristic science of our time is psychology. It is the basic human science. It marks the break between the physical sciences and the human or social sciences. It registers the fact both of continuity with sciences like biology and physiology and of discontinuity in the emergence of a new and unique subject matter.

This subject matter is man, his nature as a psycho-physical

[11] St. Luke 11:24-26.

being, his consciousness, his motivations, his mentality, his powers of imagination and will, and his aberrations and illnesses. It is very remarkable that in a scientific age like ours, when developments both in pure and in applied science have brought forth such astonishing results and show no signs of halting, psychology should have assumed a position of such commanding centrality and prominence. The reason is not far to seek. It is that man is on his own mind. He is a problem to himself. He is acutely worried and eaten up with self-concern. He is in varying degrees sick in soul.

This imparts to psychological science, and especially to that division of it which treats of mental health and disorder, called psychiatry, a much more than academic interest. This would be true even if factors of strong emotion and faith were not present and people were able to regard psychiatry with the comparative detachment and objectivity with which they think of engineering or synthetic chemistry. There would still be the drive of personal need, as there is in relation to "material" medicine and surgery. In all ages men and women afflicted with ills of the body have thronged physicians in hope and in fear, if not always in faith.

In the case of the mind and the emotions, which is the sphere of psychiatry, there is an inevitable accentuation of the personal and subjective factors. It is the "ego," the subject, the conscious person, who is involved. The patient is at once brought into an interpersonal relation with the physician at a level involving that which to the patient is intimate, personal, and momentous. In the case of classical psychiatry or psychoanalysis this is true to an extreme degree indeed, for the heart of treatment is confession, communication of consciousness, the baring without reservation of one's inmost soul. In almost all schools of psychiatry the "confessional" element remains of the essence of therapy.

But this is not all. The acutest problems of people are ethical and religious; they have to do with conduct and meaning, with values and authority, with choices in human relations and assurance for the soul. The psychiatrist cannot escape becoming both a moralist (a lawgiver) and a priest. He cannot even function without the evocation of faith. He cannot heal without the arousal in some measure of love. Inevitably then psychology passes into religion, and religion assumes a psychiatric shape. This is true whether the physician believes with Doctor Jung that true religion is the only true psychiatry or whether he is intellectually a materialist and a determinist. He must still work by faith and love, and be to guilty and anxious souls both a keeper of conscience and a priest of divine mysteries.

All of which may give us an insight into one of the strangest and most revealing phenomena of our age. Far from being a period of cold objectivity and sober, passionless scientific logic, it is an age of faith. It has faith in many things, it is seeking in different directions, it is a scene of diverse cults. Among them all none is more flourishing in the middle class world of Western culture than psychology, and none other has a priesthood so authoritative and so powerful. By a curious sequence of developments the wheel has swung full circle. In primitive cultures the medicine man is also magician and priest. In modern culture the attempt was made to separate medicine entirely from the religious or superstitious and the priestly. The result has been the reinstatement of the primitive situation. The medicine man (psychiatrist) is again a priest. He is also threatened with being made again a magician. For the attitude of people toward the psychiatrist is not rational—not any more so than that of the faithful Catholic to his priest. It is an attitude of faith, of expectation, of hope for a miracle, of belief that somehow the psychiatrist will be able to pull strings and bring about a magical cure.

How long this new psychological faith will endure—how long it will be tolerated, we cannot be certain. It is ominous that in the totalitarian regimes there is no time for psychiatry. This was true under Hitler. The venerable Sigmund Freud had to depart from his native Vienna, the birthplace of psychiatry, and die in exile. Nor can this be simply charged up to the virulence of Nazi Anti-Semitism. Equally in the Soviet Communist order there is no room for bourgeois, individual-centered psychoanalysis. This is a luxury and an indulgence which the workers' state cannot afford and does not need. So it is held. But it is just possible that the real reason is the necessary intolerance in Communism as in any thoroughly totalitarian scheme of any rival or subsidiary religion. There can be but one religion, one cult, one priesthood; and it is a monopoly of the state.

Lest some readers feel this faith-interpretation of psychiatry is far-fetched, let us note in conclusion the proposal of an eminent psychological student and writer, Dr. H. A. Overstreet. In his recent best-seller *The Mature Mind* he advances the thesis that the master concept of maturity, which implies and is partly defined by immaturity, replaces the knowledge-ignorance concept, just as that at an earlier stage of man's development replaced the theory of good and evil. Whether the new stage which psychology has ushered in, is a final one, Dr. Overstreet does not say; but he states most clearly that the new concept of maturity-immaturity replaces the two earlier stages. Evidently as far as we know it is final.

This, we submit, is philosophical psychology. It shows that psychology today is not simply a science. It is also a faith, and a faith of substance always generates a philosophy. It is bound to claim possession of the key to the highest and fullest understanding of reality. This is exactly Overstreet's claim for psychology.

(6) EXISTENTIALISM: OR SUBJECTIVITY IN REBOUND

We turn now, by a natural transition, to the field of philosophy. Philosophy denotes thought. It works by reason. It is the attempt to know what is. This attempt must begin with particular areas of experience, with specific segments of the environing system of reality we call nature. This means that philosophy presupposes the several sciences, natural and human. Its aim is knowledge of the whole from an ultimate standpoint. This is attainable only if there is reliable clear knowledge of the various parts and aspects of universal reality.

Philosophy in the modern sense began, as we have already seen, about 600 B.C. and began as an attempt to interpret reality in terms of the crude physics of the time. The father of philosophy is Plato, who undertook to unite in his thinking about what is, both science and the inward experience of man. His master, Socrates, had recalled men to inward truth, believing that the soul of man belongs to a higher, perfect world of absolute beauty and truth. His pupil, Aristotle, was less of a transcendentalist and was content with a considerable contraction of the vision splendid. He was also more systematic, took all knowledge for his province, and became the world's first and greatest encyclopedist.

From Aristotle to the greatest German systematizer early in the nineteenth century, Hegel, rationalism reigned supreme in philosophy. True for several centuries, under the influence of Christianity, it took a back seat and was subordinated to theology. Faith was held to precede reason. "I believe in order that I may understand," was the point of view of St. Augustine; it was repeated in classic form by St. Anselm at the end of the twelfth century. But Abelard was a boy when Anselm was made Archbishop of Canterbury and ahead was a mighty rebirth of confidence in reason. This trend, which is the main stream of succeeding history, reached its climax in the massive synthesis of Hegel. For him the universe is logical and rational through and through; it is Absolute Mind, Absolute Spirit. There is no other reality.

This extraordinary triumph of intellectual mastery, as it seemed for a time in Germany and for many decades in Great Britain and the United States, was at once climax and crisis. It was the end of a tremendous development, spanning in some sense twenty-three centuries. It seemed finally to fulfill the prophecy of the Greek humanist Protagoras that man is the measure of things. It united God and man, the Infinite and the finite, not by a tenuous, single miracle as Christianity had done, but by domestication, as a natural, universal fact. The mind of man had encompassed all things, and this mind was not simply a creaturely image and pale replica, but was in essence Divine. The Infinite was fulfilling itself in the finite. God was man, and man was God.

But it *was* the end. Hegel was followed by three giants of spiritual energy, as the sequel has proved, who repudiated all his works and prophesied of strange things and stranger to come. The first was a Dane named Kierkegaard, who studied in Berlin in the wake of Hegel and whose whole soul rose in revolt at what he felt was the unconscionable presumption of mortal man. He affirmed against the ultimate heresy of Hegel the infinite qualitative distinction between God and man. He re-discovered and re-presented Christianity as a paradoxical, supra-rational, revealed truth about which every individual has to make up his mind in free, radical decision.

The second was a disciple of Hegel, a German Jew named Karl Marx. Under the influence of another disciple, Feuerbach, he decided that the master was right in his method of reasoning but wrong in his starting point and in his conclusion. The result was classical Communism, the mastermotive of which is that man must and will fashion for himself a rational and humane world.

The third rebel was Friedrich Nietzsche, a German who was more than a little mad. He was the most acute analyst as well as the boldest and most radical prophet of all. He perceived the continuity of European history and of the European mind, and the perception drove him to wild rage. He did not waste time attacking the pretensions of Hegel. He was disinterested in the revolutionary aspirations of a particular class. He attacked the ancient perversion at its root. He accused the Christ of reprehensible weakness and cowardice. He assailed without compromise the whole strategy and idealism of the Sermon on the Mount. Under the name of a pre-Christian prophet and religious founder Zarathustra or Zoroaster, he announced the demise of the Christian fraud and heralded the coming of a new, vital, uninhibited, glorious Super-man.

Beside these three protestants and existentialists, all in more or less direct reaction against Hegel and philosophy, a fourth figure must be placed. He was not directly anti-Hegelian and he was not especially a rebel. He was a great Christian, an apostle of love and an affirmer forever of life, even as he descended into the deepest pit and nethermost hell of human existence and described without reserve or apology all that he saw. He was also the acutest social analyst of them all, seeing with a terrible clarity the demonic perversion of social idealism that lay ahead and that would threaten the very foundations of the life of man. Needless to say, we refer to the great Christian and the Russian Shakespeare, Fyodor Dostoievsky, of whom Nicholas Berdyaev so beautifully wrote, that if the Russian people had done nothing else than contribute to the world Dostoievsky, they would have justified their existence.

These men cannot be called rationalists. They were lonely voices, protesting and prophesying. They were pessimists in a world carried away with optimistic experiences and dreams. They differed a great deal but they were at one in affirming a tragic depth to human existence and in summoning men nevertheless to live with courage and passion.

Today we live in a period when it is plain for all to see that reason has miscarried and that man has no choice but to accept tragedy and apparent meaninglessness in life. What answer can philosophers give to this plight? What can theologians, who for so long walked in the light of reason's day, say for themselves and God?

Some give no answer. They say that almost all past philosophy was a ludicrous mistake. It is concerned with knowing, and the truth is that we can know little. We can make some statements about immediate experience, but it is easy to be loose with words and overstep the bounds of valid propositions. The job of philosophy is to be a Semantic Watchdog and see that no metaphysical or mystical cheating takes place.

The theologian, too, may have no answer. He may be simply disillusioned and tired, and retreat into agnosticism. This for the Liberal is surely a strong temptation. Or he may say, safe in the stronghold of some Fundamentalism, or secure in the logic of an ancient Orthodoxy: "It is as was said of old; man is a fallen being; he has rebelled against his Maker; behold, God is not mocked."

But all round us an answer is being given. It is being given by artists, by philosophers, by Christians, Protestant and Catholic, by atheists (as they suppose), by soldiers, by patriots, and by lovers. It is the answer of courage, integrity, and passion in the face of anxiety, guilt, and despair. It is the affirmation of the resolve to live in the face of death and in the teeth of the fear of nothingness. It is the joyful witness of the rediscovery, amid the crash of civilizations and the ruins of reason, of the depth, the hazard, and the preciousness of human existence.

Such is the essence of what is called existentialism. It is an approach to life and destiny, which puts primary emphasis on will rather than reason, on freedom rather than determinism, on passion rather than form. Very old as an ingredient and element in the history of thought, it was first given formal statement by Kierkegaard a century ago. Early in this century it became a powerful force in philosophy, and after World War I through the prophet voice of Karl Barth it began to influence and to revolutionize Protestant theology. In this country the most influential and also balanced existentialist is Professor Paul Tillich.

The significance of existentialism is two-fold. First, it is a revealing symptom; it is a signal of transition and of shifting spiritual climate. It indicates that one age has come to an end and a new period has begun. Second, it denotes a return to deeper sources of personal being. In a world of infinite unrolling years, of immense overwhelming extent of space, of vast impersonal forces uniting ever more powerfully to create the giant mechanism of modern industrial economy, it reveals man not as shrinking up in his own eyes but as growing more aware of his uniqueness and glory. In an order of devouring objectivity, it shows us subjectivity in splendid rebound.

(7) The Rise of a New World Religion

The final and conclusive proof that a new religious age has come is the rise, spread, and threat of a new universal salvation religion—Communism.

Communism, as we have already seen, can only be understood if it is seen as a world religion, not lacking in a Semitic tinge, in many respects paralleling or caricaturing Christianity, of a strongly dogmatic, authoritarian, and intolerant type. This fact makes doubly significant the origin of Communism. It arose as a development and offshoot of nineteenth century rationalism. This genesis is not of its essence. As we have already seen, Marx was in reaction against the Olympian idealism of his teacher Hegel. He broke, in reality, with the philosophical tradition, but the break was less violent and diametrical than that made by Kierkegaard and by Nietzsche. A number of rational elements were retained in the new Marxist system and are incorporated still, in theory, in the Communist world-view.

Furthermore, what Marx attempted to do was to give socialism a scientific basis. Reason is the instrument of science, and science rests upon the belief that the world is a rational order. Communism is at this point closely parallel in origin with democracy, capitalism, and liberalism. This makes its ultimate deviation and radical religious transformation all the more striking.

Summary

Such are the basic fields of fact which seem to be signs and evidences of the coming of a new age. They indicate that a distinctive historical period is already well under way. This period will differ sharply from the Age of Reason and Science. It will be dominated not by immanent reason and individual self-reliance but by outreaching faith and the quest for salvation.

So far the new period, which we believe was definitely ushered in by World War I, has been a time of destruction and woe, of calamity and terror. We have become hardened and inured to the spectacle of human tragedy and degradation. We have become "punch-drunk," as it were, and hardly register, as our eyes run over the newest chronicle in newspaper or illustrated weekly magazine of man's fearful and truly unbelievable inhumanity to man. It may be that future generations will look back to our time and to us who inhabited then the world, and say, "Ah! They lived through that time of infernal horror and of more than apocalyptic bestiality, when the famed Four Horsemen seemed like friends, and civilized, rational men outdid their own worst dreams of demons and fiends."

MENACE AND PROMISE

The First World War was followed in less than a generation by a Second—on a more universal, more sanguinary, and more destructive scale, especially as regarded the civil populations of the contending powers. This War has brought not peace and reconciliation, but something new in mankind's long history—continuing, remorseless, undeclared Cold War. The new war is primarily between the two most powerful allies of World War II, and is ideological and religious in character. It is the result of the boldest, most calculated, most determined, and most unscrupulous bid for world supremacy ever made. The goal is not land or riches or empire or worldly splendor, at least in any primary sense. The goal is nothing less than the souls of men. It is a spiritual empire. It is nothing less than the formation of a single international monolithic world community, ruled over by a new hierarchical priesthood, the inner circle of the Communist party, which itself represents the Chosen People of History, the Proletariat.

Knowing all this and facing the gravest threat of all history, realizing the enormous price we have to pay for transition from one age to another, we may wonder what lies ahead. We may question the worthwhileness of the onward voyage. Yet we know that this is the way of history and that there have been many times of darkness in ages past. It may be that behind the hideous cloud which now covers almost the whole horizon, the sun is shining and the land is bright. It may be that there an age lies concealed which has promise of some mighty and surprising fulfillment.

III

The Christian Revolution

If any man be in Christ, he is a new creation.
—II Cor. 5:17

IT IS RECORDED in the first Church History ever to be written, *The Acts of the Apostles,* that out in the Greek city of Thessalonica a mob of vile fellows was incited to storm the house of a convert named Jason. The aim was to catch Paul and Silas and tear them apart. When these worthies were not found, poor Jason and certain brethren who were fellow-Christians, were dragged before the rulers of the city. At this point the rabble shouted:

These that have turned the world upside down are come hither also; whom Jason hath received: and these all do contrary to the decrees of Caesar, saying that there is another king, one Jesus.[1]

"These that have turned the world upside down!" It was true. Actually the poor ignorant vile fellows of the mob were guilty of a great understatement of the case, though they could never have known this. Jesus Christ brought into the world something incredibly dynamic. He brought not only a sword, deliberately disturbing the world's peace. He brought spiritual dynamite. He inaugurated permanent revolution. He let loose a spirit of indomitable agitation and disturbance. Centuries later in the midst of the storm and confusion of the French Revolution, this higher truth was revealed to a great Christian seer, prophet, and poet.

[1] Acts 17:6, 7.

> Bring me my bow of burning gold!
> Bring me my arrows of desire!
> Bring me my spear! O clouds, unfold!
> Bring me my chariot of fire!
>
> I will not cease from mental fight,
> Nor shall my sword sleep in my hand,
> Till we have built Jerusalem
> In England's green and pleasant land.

And so in all lands, and in the whole earth. So in the realms under the earth and between earth and heaven.

> Thy Kingdom come. Thy will be done, on earth as it is in heaven.

> For he must reign, till he hath put all enemies under his feet. The last enemy that shall be destroyed is death.[2]

> And upon this rock I will build my church; and the gates of Hades [the abode of the dead] shall not prevail against it.[3]

CHRISTIANITY—A SPIRITUAL REVOLUTION

Yes, Christianity was a spiritual revolution, destined to produce first a psychological revolution and then in time a social and scientific revolution. It was destined to produce a revolution in creation itself. A new man, a new outlook, a new society, were to result. And, please God!, the Christian Revolution is not finished. Ahead is a brighter light, a better world, greater things for man, a consummation in this order worthy of the Lord Jesus Christ and pleasing to God our Creator and Father.

There is a verse in the letters of that difficult but extraordinary genius St. Paul, which states most clearly the character of the Christian Revolution.

> Therefore, if any one is in Christ, he is a new creation; the old has passed away, behold, the new has come.[4]

[2] I Cor. 15:25, 26.
[3] St. Matt. 16:18, RV.
[4] II Corinthians 5:17, RSV.

In these stirring words the Apostle describes Christianity from the manward side—from the angle of its meaning for human experience and existence. He does not speak immediately of God, or of Christ the Son and perfect image of the Father, or of the Holy Spirit or Divine Breath of God, or even of the Cross and Resurrection, though these are in the background and are close at hand. What Paul speaks of is man and of what has happened to man because of Christ. He says that Christ brings a new power and reality of being. He says that if any person is in Christ, that is, sees the meaning of Christ's life and death and resurrection and is drawn into that meaning, the result is a new creation. Old, fearful, paralyzing, death-dealing things pass away; new, fresh, creative, out-reaching, victorious things take their place.

LOVE AND NEW BEING

Only one force known and experienced by human beings could possibly bring about such a remaking of man's nature and sense of destiny. Arbitrary power could not; intoxication —the wine-god Bacchus—could not; the intellectual faculties could not. Neither could artistic creativity, nor the worship of nature, nor the pleasure of the senses.

Love alone is able to change and transform and recreate man. Without it we are sure—on the basis of human experience alone—there can be no new creation. There can be no new being. There can be no death to that which is anxious and old; there can be no birth to that which is everlastingly fresh and divinely new. For love is the only thing that ever engages one's whole self and at the same time takes one entirely outside self.

This is the mystery of natural being. This is the unerased aboriginal stamp of the Divine image in man. This is the preparation for the coming into the world of God—in the form of a servant named Jesus Christ.

The drama of Christ is the drama of human and Divine love. It is the story, enacted in a real human life, at a definite time in history, on a particular bit of the earth's surface, of the assertion, the rejection, and the triumph of perfect love. Here we have summarized the three acts of the play that was also Reality.

ASSERTION OF LOVE IN CHRIST

The assertion of love we see in the life of Christ and in His intuitive, life-associated knowledge of God's character and ways. The key-phrase here, often on His lips, is "the will of God." Where others chose their own wills, Christ chose a higher will—that of the unchanging Father in Heaven. Where others were greedy and grasping, He emptied Himself. Where others strove for prestige and power, He was meek and selfless. Where others lashed out and struck back, He forgave and blessed. Where others sought to destroy, He sought to build. His disciples, He declared, were not to be as the great men of the Gentiles, lovers of power and tenacious of prerogative, lording it over all underlings and lesser breeds. Instead they were to be servants and slaves of all, holding this and this alone to be greatness, even as the Son of man Himself "came not to be served but to serve, and to give his life as a ransom for many."[5]

In another connection He drew a sharp contrast between the life of men ordinarily and the quality of His followers. Here His thought includes not only the Romans and their minions but His own people the Jews and the ancient law of Moses.

[5] St. Mark 10:45, RSV.

You have heard . . . An eye for an eye and a tooth for a tooth . . .
You have heard . . . You shall love your neighbor and hate your
enemy. But I say . . . Love your enemies and pray for those who
persecute you, so that you may be sons of your Father who is in
heaven; for he makes his sun rise on the evil and on the good, and
sends rain on the just and on the unjust. For if you love those who love
you, what reward have you? Do not even the tax collectors do the
same? And if you salute only your brethren, what more are you
doing than others? Do not even the Gentiles do the same? You,
therefore, must be perfect, as your heavenly Father is perfect.[6]

Men were, of course, unable to tolerate such a love. They
sensed at once, as we would were our ears and hearts not
dulled by familiarity, the revolutionary character of such
doctrine. And it was not a doctrine merely—it was not a
closet speculation or even a rabbi's refinement in a school
of the law where as in all schools many nice distinctions
have to be made but where it is commonly understood that
nothing is to be taken too seriously.

Instead this teaching was set forth with the strongest
claim of authority. It superseded, said Jesus, the law given
Moses on Mount Sinai. But even this might have been let
pass. There are many fanatics, many visionaries, many
pseudo-prophets, many egomaniacs. Jesus, however, did more.
He did the ultimate thing. "In the beginning was the deed."
He embodied the new doctrine in his own person. He lived
it out with absolute freedom, fearlessness, and transcendence
of self-concern.

THE REJECTION OF LOVE

So He became, as was inevitable, a shining target for envy,
hatred, malice, cruelty, pride, presumption, and hypocrisy.
Love was rejected. It was rejected not with mildness but with

[6] St. Matt. 5:38, 43-48, RSV.

angry scorn and wild rage. He who had asserted Love without any limit, was seized, abused, tortured, and executed. He was nailed to a tree.

Now comes the supreme miracle. This should have been the end. The Christ had failed. His love had been rejected. His revolutionary claim to be the rightful King and Lord of men had had no material force behind it, and He was wiped out, liquidated, given the desert of a madman and a nuisance.

Yet this was not the end at all. It was the beginning of the mightiest triumph in history. There was a third act, which is still going on, the victory of Love.

Assertion . . . . rejection! But the Christ did not accept rejection. He maintained even at the moment of complete rejection, utter loss, absolute hopelessness, the love which He had ascribed to God Himself and had enjoined so firmly upon His disciples. This was the decisive moment. This was the point of Jesus' certain manifestation as the Christ. This was the beginning of the triumph of Love.

The Triumph of Love

"He reigns from the tree." He is Lord from the Crucifix. Only a crucified Christ could be truly Christ. The Good Shepherd is the one who lays down his life for the sheep. Love to be fully asserted must be completely rejected. Never can Christ the Lord come down from His Cross.

This of course is only one part of the Victory of Love. Another mighty event occurred. Death was overthrown, along with hatred and the will to destroy and the lust of revenge. Death and Hell were trampled upon when Love was fully asserted; Life and Immortality were brought to light. Resurrection is the Christian symbol of God's deed of vindication, necessary to show vicious crucifiers, compromising washers of the hands of responsibility, cowardly deniers of the Lord of Love, then and now, that Christ is not a transient flash of lightning illumining for a brief moment the mystery of our being, but is one Reality and Substance with the Father. His victory is for all time and beyond time. He is the Resurrection and the Life as well as the Way and the Truth.

LOVE AND DEATH

This final teaching of Christianity, which might be called God's personal certification of the Christian Revolution, has an interesting parallel and fore-type in natural love. If the poets may be taken as true interpreters of experience, and by common consent this is one of the supreme tests of poetry, there is a deep affinity between Love and Death. Some of the greatest poetry, for example, of Shelley and Keats, the premier poets of the Romantic Movement, is charged with an intense sense of this interconnection of two ultimate realities.

> I arise from dreams of thee
>   In the first sweet sleep of night,
> When the winds are breathing low,
>   And the stars are shining bright.
>   * * *
> The wandering airs they faint
>   On the dark, the silent stream,—
> The champak odors fail
>   Like sweet thoughts in a dream;
>   * * *
> O, lift me from the grass!
>   I die, I faint, I fail!
> Let thy love in kisses rain
>   On my lips and eyelids pale.

My cheek is cold and white, alas!
My heart beats loud and fast:
O, press it close to thine again,
Where it will break at last![7]

Darkling I listen; and, for many a time
I have been half in love with easeful Death,
Call'd him soft names in many a muséd rhyme,
To take into the air my quiet breath;
Now more than ever seems it rich to die,
To cease upon the midnight with no pain,
While thou art pouring forth thy soul abroad
In such an ecstasy!
Still wouldst thou sing, and I have ears in vain—
To thy high requiem become a sod.[8]

No—yet still stedfast, still unchangeable,
Pillow'd upon my fair love's ripening breast,
To feel for ever its soft fall and swell,
Awake for ever in a sweet unrest,
Still, still to hear her tender-taken breath.
And so live ever—or else swoon to death.[9]

From a psychological standpoint it is evident that in moods such as these verses reflect we are in the presence of the Death-urge, identified by Sigmund Freud and presented by him as the closely related polar opposite of the Will to Live or Life-wish. Often the balance between these two currents of the deep unconscious Psyche is very delicate, and it is evident that Love, rooted in Libido or sexual desire but in no case to be simply and flatly identified with this organic drive, is deeply intertwined with both. According to our

[7] Shelley, *Indian Serenade.*
[8] Keats, *Ode to the Nightingale.*
[9] Keats, Sonnet: *Bright Star.*

development and experience in love, the scale is tipped toward Death or Life. In poets like William Blake and Robert Browning (to choose two who are very different from each other) we have an extremely powerful affirmation of life. And as it is with poets, so it is with all of us. Before every soul is the choice of Life or Death, and in every soul there are hidden, secret forces influencing the decision that has finally to be made. But there is also in every normal person some margin of freedom—an area of opportunity for determining by knowledge and purpose the act of choosing.

LIFE—AFFIRMATION OF CHRIST

It is here that the figure of Christ and the religion called by His name are seen to be of the highest importance to every man. Christ was, as William Blake declared, the bright preacher of life. His life-affirmation is the clearest and strongest of which we have any record. It, in turn, is rooted and grounded in the wholeness, fulness, and maturity of His love —expressed in attitude to man and in portrayal of God.

If Christ is reality, and in appealing to this conclusion we are standing entirely within the confines of experience and public matter of fact, there is no reason to suppose that life is finally overcome by death. On the contrary, there is every presumption of the immortality of love. And in the fact that Christianity as a world religion began because of the faith of the Resurrection, there is a wonderful fitness.

Love, life, resurrection, immortality—this is the Christian sequence. Let it not be said that there is here any issue of spiritual dope—of pie in the sky by and by—, for Christ lived on earth in the here and now and whatever He has to teach and give us applies to life as we know it and live it. The Cross and Resurrection have no meaning for us unless we experience them now as "death and life" realities. Unless we come out now on the side of life, we shall not desire life beyond and we should not know what to do with it if it were given us. Yet apart from the full Resurrection faith of orthodox Christianity, a dark shadow overhangs the universe, and obscures the being and the power of God.

GOSPEL OF THE RESURRECTION

This is the reconciliation of the momentousness of life here and the Gospel of the Resurrection. This is the answer to modern men and women who say they are not concerned about a future life. Thoreau, the fanatical individualist of Concord, was wrong about a great many things, but he was more right than the Evangelical preacher pestering him on his death-bed about the state of his soul, when he retorted: "One world at a time, brother: one world at a time!" Yet in the end the man who has loved and lived greatly, who has entered into the shadow of Christ's Cross and seen the glory of His Resurrection, cannot dismiss "the life of the world to come." He cannot doubt—any more than the Apostles in the first century—that He who was Perfect Love is alive, is the Lord, and is a King of whose Kingdom there shall be no end.

Such is the Christ. Such is the material of the new creation of man in Him. Such is the shape and form of the Christian Revolution in the first century and in the twentieth. We turn now to the analysis of what the actual effect of this radically new outlook was in history. Did a new man make his appearance in the world?

A SECOND MODERN QUERY

Before we turn, however, to this factual theme, let us face a question that disturbs the minds of many who have read down to this point. What we have said so far is impressive. It brings the reality of Christ into connection with life as we live it. It raises issues that are tremendously interesting and vital to every thoughtful man and woman. But is not such a view of Christ somewhat unreal? Is it not a bit mythological? Are we not simply taking material in the Gospels and ingeniously constructing an ideal figure—a Prince after all of a Fairy Story—or of a psychologically purified Romance?

This is a query which cannot be airily dismissed. It cannot be answered simply and dogmatically. The answer is one that we must give personally as we confront the Christ of the New Testament, using fully the very great aids of modern scholarship, and as we in turn are confronted by Him. We shall also be helped to see the truth of Christ as we face and master the facts of history, of psychology, of the present crisis of human existence. Here is one example of an understanding of Christ that comes out of a major field of study, experiment, and application—psychological and psychiatric science. This passage from a German psychiatrist of Jewish birth and up-bringing is one of the most exciting things I have come across in a long time. It may suggest an answer to the mythological query which so haunts the mind of our time.

Looking at the history of the human spirit at long range, it is a tremendous thing that psychoanalysis has rediscovered the primary position of love in Man's world. This discovery was made from a materialist platform, as it were. What else could we expect from a genius who is a child of the nineteenth century? Lop a few of the accidental ornaments off and you have a psychology which reaffirms and enriches the Christian idea of Man. Psychoanalysis gives us an embryology of love. Christianity could make use of this very thing. Psychoanalysis shows us that the infant is more of a passive recipient of love than an active lover, and that it cannot bear hostility. As we become more mature, we are more able to love actively and we learn to be able to be rejected. Christianity teaches us that the climax of human perfection is to love infinitely to be able to be hated infinitely. This degree of human maturity has been reached perhaps only once in history, in the person of Jesus Christ. Psychoanalysis teaches us that *Amor* can be transformed into *Caritas*. So does Christianity. Later generations will see that in the rediscovery of the crude archaic traces of "love" in Man's physical nature, there occurs a decisive turning-away from the Manichaeism of which Western Man has been so dangerously ill.[10]

A New Historical Man

Now we turn to history. We leave aside all speculation, all psychological reconstruction, all analysis of present experience and faith. We ask, what happened to man after Christ came into the world? Was St. Paul a prophet when he declared that the man who is in Christ is a new creation? Did he stumble, as in the ecstasy and exultation of faith he strove to voice for himself and others the meaning of Christ, upon the key to succeeding history, not for a few decades or even centuries, but for two millenniums? I believe that the Apostle did just this, and that in his idea of the new creation in Christ we have a summary of man in history ever since, coming right down to the vast climax and crisis of human existence in our time.

A convenient point of departure is the following passage, which we shall not identify, but which was penned not long before the year 1600 and which occurs in probably the most influential single work ever composed in the English language. This work incidentally is as up-to-date today as it was three centuries ago.

[10] Stern, *The Pillar of Fire* (New York, Harcourt, Brace & Company) pp. 278-279.

. . . . I have of late, —but wherefore I know not, —lost all my mirth,
forgone all custom of exercises; and, indeed, it goes so heavily with
my disposition that this goodly frame, the earth, seems to me a sterile
promontory; this most excellent canopy, the air, look you, this brave
o'erhanging firmament, this majestical roof fretted with golden fire,
—why, it appears no other thing to me than a foul and pestilent
congregation of vapours. What a piece of work is man! How noble
in reason! how infinite in faculties! in form and moving, how express
and admirable! in action, how like an angel! in apprehension, how
like a god! the beauty of the world! the paragon of animals! And yet,
to me, what is this quintessence of dust? man delights not me; no,
nor woman neither, ...

Besides this passage, which is the keenest as well as the
most delicately balanced and gorgeously phrased summary
we have of Renaissance man, we place another written
toward the end of his life by the same poet and put most
appropriately in the mouth of a woman.

> O, wonder!
> How many goodly creatures are there here!
> How beauteous mankind is! O brave new world!
> That hath such people in't!

This passage suggests even in phraseology the thought of
St. Paul: "If any one . . . he is a new creation; the old has
passed away, behold, the new has come." There are, however,
two momentous differences.

First, the application in the later statement is social, not
merely individual. And it is assumed that as man is, so is his
world. "How beauteous mankind is! O brave new world!"
From this standpoint the speech of Miranda is the perfect
prophecy of the history that is to come.

Secondly, the words "in Christ," which we deleted inten-
tionally in quoting a moment ago our key-text from St. Paul,
is absent from the thought of Shakespeare in both of the

passages in question. And the omission is unintentional. It is, therefore, ominous and pregnant in significance. *It means that we are in the presence of a new historical man. A new creation has emerged. A man has arisen in time with a new consciousness, a new set of assumptions about self, the world, and society, a new outlook on life, a new belief in God, and a new confidence in himself.*

Such a result did not come about in a day. It was a plant of slow growth. The soil in which it grew was Christian soil; the sun from which it had derived constant energy was the Sun of a new righteousness, arisen in Christ with healing in his wings; and the rain which watered it across not a few centuries was the gentle rain falling from a new, more clearly conceived, more certain heaven. The planter, or in old language, the husbandman was God in Christ, God known as the Lover and Liberator of man.

The characteristic traits of the mature plant, the new man in history, are freedom, the sense of rationality, confidence, optimism, the consciousness of being at home in the universe. The universe indeed has come to be thought of unconsciously as God's house of many mansions, rational and home-like through and through. Earth is a part of the whole and is man's mother with whom he is happy and free. There is a great deal in man's normal mentality of the sense of sonship, of inheritance as an heir of all things, of divinity itself. After the Renaissance, though there are ups and downs, ebbs and flows, in the tide of history, this is destined to become a full-blown doctrine of man, reaching its climax in the nineteenth century. The heart of this doctrine, theologically stated, is that every man is a natural Christ.

Such a stream of social consciousness is bound to have many expressions. Even naturalism and materialism become different. Communism, for example, is atheistic and materialistic, but it has a great deal of the new idea of man. German National Socialism professed a naturalistic theism in opposition to the Communist materialism, and identified God with nature. Man it regarded as the offspring of this nature-god,—subject to the divine commandments defined as the laws of nature. Adolf Hitler was the prophet and messiah of this pitilessly logical, absurdly inconsistent modernist religion. Liberalism, as distinct from liberality, or liberal as an adjective with a lower case "l," was shot through with the notion of the divinity of man. In Liberal Christianity there is the same view, always a little qualified. In Emerson and New England Transcendentalism, and in Mrs. Eddy and Christian Science, we have the real climax religiously of the naturalization and secularization of the Christian redemption.

Proof to Be Found in Greek Man

The proof that this is a correct account of modern man and that a new creation really took place in time, is the outlook and consciousness of the Greeks. We choose them from among all ancient peoples because of their unique modernity in their own time and their abiding subsequent influence. Hebraism is the progenitor of Christianity and there is an organic continuity between the two. Even so, it is evident that Judaism remains a particularized religion, linked with a single race and tradition, without the potential creativity and universal appeal of Christianity.

When at that notable "rebirth" we call the Renaissance, when man felt that he had shaken off old shackles and entered into a new world, he was under a strong inspiration. The thing that attracted him, that he felt was moving him, and that he desired to recover was the intellect and art of

Greek antiquity. It was, in the words of a later poet, "the glory that was Greece, and the grandeur that was Rome," but especially the first. Beside the dream of antique splendor and beauty, the past seemed to Renaissance man, as it often does to an individual personality from adolescence through the middle twenties or even longer, flat, sterile, and barbarous. The old had passed, the new had come. The stimulus, however, came, as again often with an individual, from something with a long tradition, misty and hoary with age.

SENSE OF FINITENESS

Actually, the Greek was a being radically different from the new historical man. He was, above all things, characterized by a sense of finiteness and limitation. For him reason meant the wisdom to keep within bounds, not the capacity of indefinite fulfillment and achievement. Aristotle is a striking illustration. He is the rationalist *par excellence*. He is also the chief inspiration of the Middle Ages. The great historian of Christian dogma, von Harnack, sums up the broad sweep of Mediaeval development in the vivid formula: "Augustine falls; Aristotle rises." The poet Dante referred to the latter as "the master of those who know." Yet Aristotle is the exemplar of the Golden Mean. His motto is, "nothing in excess." He is the apostle of measure and moderation.

Would it be an exaggeration to say that modern man by comparison has been characterized by immoderation and the absence of a consciousness of inherent limitation?

SENSE OF MORTALITY

A second trait of Greek man is his haunting sense of mortality. For him change was not something to cheer and lift the spirit. It was a source of melancholy. It spelled decay and loss. It caught and took down into nothingness all beauteous forms, all gracious shapes, all order and proportion imposed momentarily by the persuasion of reason upon the enveloping chaos of eternal not-being.

The essential Greek feeling was very like that of the nineteenth century Anglican parson and hymnodist, H. F. Lyte:

> Change and decay in all around I see;
> O Thou who changest not, abide with me.

The poet Keats also understood this feeling, but he did more. He understood the Greek attempt to mitigate the loss, to arrest the inevitable tragedy, by capturing in plastic art the forms most beautiful.

> Heard melodies are sweet, but those unheard
>   Are sweeter; therefore, ye soft pipes, play on;
> Not to the sensual ear, but, more endear'd,
>   Pipe to the spirit ditties of no tone:
> Fair youth, beneath the trees, thou canst not leave
>   Thy song, nor ever can those trees be bare;
>   Bold Lover, never, never canst thou kiss,
> Though winning near the goal—yet, do not grieve;
>   She cannot fade, though thou hast not thy bliss,
>   For ever wilt thou love, and she be fair!
> * * * * *
> O Attic shape! Fair attitude! with brede
>   Of marble men and maidens overwrought,
> With forest branches and the trodden weed;
>   Thou, silent form, dost tease us out of thought
> As doth eternity: . . .[11]

Keats was captured by the Greek strain which was far from absent in the nineteenth century. In addition, he had a poet's imagination and he lived for a considerable time at the height of his young powers in the presence of certain ap-

[11] *Ode on a Grecian Urn.*

proaching death. The characteristic modern man is very different. He is unaware of death in any deep, oppressive sense. It has no terrors for his optimism. It is either removed by a doctrine of natural, universal immortality, or it is pushed back by medical science and more immediate constructive interests, or it is dismissed as not really important.

The controlling element is the outlook on change, which in turn is expressive of basic world-view or concept of the Real. For the modern man change is not an evil. It does not spell decay. It is the form of achievement, of growth, of progress. The source of this outlook is the Bible and Christianity. It is most definitely not Greece or the Greeks.

DUALISM

A third trait of Greek man is his divided sense about the Universe. For him Reality is not all one thing. The Ultimate is not of one piece. There is the Good, and there is also the Evil. There is the Beautiful and it is grounded in everlasting Order, but there is also the ultimately Ugly, the unconquerable final Disorder or Chaos or Not-being. Evil is eternal; it is rooted in primal matter; and the world, being partly composed of matter, cannot be redeemed.

This explains the Greek outlook on history—so innately pessimistic and so alien to the modern spirit. For the Greek reason is a very great reality. It is active; it has a splendid foothold in man; its victory is manifest in the rise and flowering of civilizations. But the triumph is always temporary, and it is unwise to hope for too much. The blind brute force inherent in things will have its inning, and over-turn the fairest achievements of men and gods.

For the Greek, therefore, there could be no over-arching purpose or goal in history. Instead he held the cyclic view, involving the idea of an infinite succession of worlds, each developing along more or less similar lines and in the end meeting the same tragic fate. The German Spengler in his *Decline of the West,* produced at the close of World War I, revived the old Greek conception of history and dressed it up in scientific clothes.

Modern Faith in History

All this is in the strongest contrast to the outlook generated at the Renaissance and held with a continual increase of faith until our own time. For modern man there is nothing in reality that offers resistance to reason. There is nothing to inhibit or to defeat an ever enlarging good. At first it was nature that man set out to master. Then it was society and history. Reinhold Niebuhr has argued that the real faith of modern man is faith in history. It has the promise and meaning of existence. It takes the place of God.

Underlying this faith, however, is a conception of the Real. It is the conception given classical statement by Hegel, that the real is the rational, and the rational is the real. There is nothing else. Evil disappears as a fundamental element in the Universe. The whole world is the expression of a single principle. History is no longer meaningless (as with the Greeks and the Hindus). It is no longer a tale of two cities (as with Augustine who brought into classical synthesis the Christian sense of the reality of evil and Christ's doctrine of the Kingdom of Heaven). It is the march of absolute Spirit. It is the finite manifestation of infinite fulfillment and absolute perfection.

Such a view is heretical from the standpoint of Christianity. It has done much harm. It lulled men into a false sense of security and laid the ground for the volcanic eruptions of evil that characterize our century. Yet it could never have come into existence save in a Christian culture. It is a fruit of the change in outlook brought about by Jesus Christ. It is the expression of a new historical man—a creation without precedent in past ages. For this man the old had passed away; all things were new and fair and divine.

DEMOCRACY—ANCIENT AND MODERN

This gives us the background of the rise and spread of modern democracy. It is impossible to understand this unique development unless it is clearly realized that man had accepted a new view of himself, of his world, and of the course of history. The architects of revolution and of republicanism on novel lines in North America near the close of the eighteenth century, believed that their experiment represented a decisive turning point in human history and lighted the way for all generations to come. This faith was not without antecedents. It did not just happen. It was a secular expression of the Christian experience of a new creation.

Democracy as a form of government was not new when Thomas Jefferson drafted the Declaration of Independence. More than two thousand years before the Greek City States had experimented extensively with government by assembly of all the citizens. In Athens pure democracy of this sort had had a glorious period, although it had proven unstable and weak in grave emergencies. It was tarnished also by its close connection with the institution of slavery, accepted as a matter of course by all Athenians in common with the ancients generally.

In Rome, which had begun as a city state, democracy was not unknown. The assembly of the people was, however, but one element in Roman government, for Rome remained stable and became a great world power by virtue of the mixed constitution its leaders were able to devise. This "combine" type of state framework, drawing together democratic, aristocratic, and monarchical elements of rule, was the prototype of the American Constitution. Hamilton, Madison, and Adams were consciously influenced by the precedent of Rome, and our Constitution represented originally a free imitation of Roman republicanism, with the House of Representatives taking the place of the ancient assembly of the people.

Neither Greece nor Rome, however, explains democracy as we know it. Significantly also it arose more than three centuries later than the new birth of the European Renaissance. *Democracy in its modern form is a doctrine of man before it is a form of government. It is a spirit, a mentality, a consciousness much more than a mechanism of rule.* It arose as a revolutionary force when the new man, secure in his world and assured of the adequacy of his powers of reason and freedom, turned from nature and her secrets to society and its problems.

The period of Revolution began in England. It was initiated as an assertion of Christian freedom by children of the Protestant Reformation—the Puritans. The more radical Independents, led by Cromwell, were similar in theological outlook. They were more against tyranny than for freedom, except for themselves and like-minded Christians. The result was speedy reaction and the restoration of the House of Stuart.

The real English revolution came bloodlessly in 1688 when the stiff-necked Stuarts were finally cast out. It was a limited, aristocratic affair. But it had one very far-reaching result. It caused the greatest philosopher of the day, John Locke, to turn his mind and pen to the subject of politics and civil government.

Locke held the new Renaissance view of man. He thought of man as free, independent, rational—an autonomous self-sufficient individual. Man for Locke is not in any sense the product of social forces, but is himself the creator of society. Society is a compact made by free individuals, and the State is a further special arrangement worked out within Society. The right of revolution clearly followed, and Locke's logical vindication of the supremacy of Parliament and the overthrow of the Stuarts was highly acclaimed.

The sequel was not so palatable to those in authority in England or elsewhere. The sequel was the *Declaration of Independence* of 1776 and the successful American Revolution. The *Declaration* was largely a rearrangement and adaptation of the ideas of Locke, with some liberalization on the primacy of property as a natural right. This, however, is unimportant. Locke was not really original, but was the mouthpiece of ideas whose time had come. He expressed the self-consciousness of the new historical man. This man by comparison with ancient man is a new creation. He thinks of himself as by his very nature an heir of God, a joint-heir with Christ, a partaker of the Divine nature, a spirit at home in the house of his Father's creation, a free being endowed with inalienable natural rights.

The *Declaration* is a universal document, voicing the same ideas, instinct with the same consciousness. It projects a society to be run on new lines and to serve new ends—ends of man as man, the majestic designs of liberty and equality for all, the hope of deliverance for ever from tyranny and oppression. *The vision of such a society inspired the American Revolution. It is the meaning of American democracy and of all striving for a democratic way of life. Democracy is the dream of the new creation in society. It is an extension of the Christian Revolution.*

TOTALITARIAN REACTION

Today, as we have seen, reaction in a gigantic pattern has set in. Democracy, the Christian tradition, all freedom, are threatened by the oldest, toughest, and craftiest of the totalitarian systems. This system, entrenched in Russia, in power in China, and now it may be on its way to seize all Asia, is called Communism. It comes to men not as a vicious design for enslaving first the souls and then the bodies of men, but in the guise of an angel of light. It comes as a new religion, as a faith that restores meaning to life and to history, as a Gospel of deliverance. It appeals not merely to the base in man, but also to his idealism and sense of community with others. In reality it is the religion of the man-god in almost unadulterated form, and represents with terrible precision the fulfillment of the direst prophecies of Dostoievsky and Tolstoy three quarters of a century ago.

DEMOCRACY AS A FAITH

But democracy is also threatened from within. Its inner vitality is undermined and its resistance to the viruses of unbelief, materialism, greed, and sensationalism is dangerously low. Democracy is a doctrine of man. It is a sense of the dignity and worth of man as man. It is faith in the value of the individual human person. This faith, as we have seen, did not just happen. It is Biblical and Christian in origin. It became a power in history because man after generations had been so indoctrinated with Christian ideas that they became a part of his integral, natural consciousness.

Faith in man, however, never stands alone—at least for long. Faith in every form is related to some general doctrine of Reality—some outlook and view of the whole. In the case of democracy we have to do with a faith which began not with man but with God and with the recreation of man's nature in Christ. This was the astounding thing that Christianity did—to give man a new grip, a new courage, a new outlook, a new sense of himself. This happened because of the love of God asserted without limit in Jesus Christ. But it was so real and powerful and pervasive that the new creation of which St. Paul speaks in II Corinthians became man's normal view of himself. A new historical man emerged, and brought in modern history, including science, democracy, and one must add—Socialism and Communism.

Today man in the free world as well as in the darkness behind the iron curtain is in danger of losing all sense of his spiritual inheritance. For the masses as well as intellectuals and leaders the drift is toward the loss of any doctrine of Reality that undergirds and supports the faith of democracy. The phrase "in Christ" is not only without meaning; there is no belief left in the God of Jesus Christ, and the world is regarded not as a Divine construction but as a mammoth machine hurtling through infinite space without origin, direction or purpose.

OPPORTUNITY FOR AMERICA

This trend is less advanced in America than elsewhere. Our country remains basically a grass-roots affair, with the Christian religion in some form a powerful element in the up-bringing and often the later life of the multitudes. Because of many special elements in our history and culture we have an extraordinary aptitude for combining the material and the spiritual, the secular and the Biblical, the practical and the ideal. This combination, in many respects, is America. It explains our growth and greatness. It is the key to the power and persistence of our democratic faith. It is the partial explanation of our destiny as the champion of freedom over against Russo-Communist imperialism in the twentieth century day of Armageddon. It gives hope for the revival of faith in our nervous world and for the renewal of God's recreative power in Christ.

But the hour is short. Opportunity does not knock for ever. There is a tide in the things of the spirit as well as those of might and power. If seized, it leads on to fulness and victory; if missed, there is no undoing the disaster of loss and defeat, so far as we are concerned.

America has today the mightiest opportunity in history. It is not merely the chance to throw back the forces of reaction and to repel the evil and demonic dream of a single, man-governed totalitarian world. Nothing negative will suffice. Simple condemnation will not stem the tide of a dynamic advance. Humanity, said the late General Smuts, has struck its tents, and is on the march. The opportunity of our great country, which God has so wonderfully led and so richly blessed, is to lead faltering mankind beyond the twilight and the hovering darkness into the sunshine of a larger and happier day. It is to use our vast resources and inspiring inheritance under God to usher the whole earth into a period of abundance, freedom, and brotherhood. It is to be a strategic agent in continuing God's recreative work in Christ. It is to extend and ever more to consolidate in the affairs of men the Christian Revolution.

IV

Jesus Christ and the American Way

Ye shall know the truth, and the truth shall make you free.
—St. John 8:32.
Jesus saith. . . . I am the way, the truth, and the life.
—St. John 14:6.

ON JULY 4, 1951, Americans everywhere celebrated the 175th Anniversary of the Declaration of Independence. Much was written in the press and said over radio and television about the Declaration. It was quoted ten thousand times and more, and in many varied contexts. A great deal was said about the American way. Some analysis of this was offered, principally in terms quoted from the *Declaration*. In the main orators and editorialists concentrated on expressing with eloquence their approval of the American way and exhorting Americans to be more mindful of the privileges which they enjoy.

Not much was said on the Fourth of July about Jesus Christ. Christianity and Christian civilization may have come in for occasional mention, but this was certainly exceptional. In no case was there a disposition to consider the Christian way and its relation to the American way.

In one respect this is not surprising. There is a kind of generally accepted tabu on religion in public discussion. This is partly a general state of mind which is habituated to the thought of religion as an entirely private affair. It is partly the result of the separation of Church and State understood, as it is by so many million Americans, as the separation of the State and religion.

DEMOCRACY AND SPIRITUAL RENEWAL

Yet as a fact of history democracy in its modern form derives from Christianity. It has arisen in no other culture or religious tradition. The crises in which it finds itself today is in large part expressive of the decline and decay in the West as a whole of vital Christian faith. This decline has been less marked in the United States than in any other country and democracy in consequence is more virile here than anywhere else. Indeed American democracy is an offspring of which the great mother Christianity need not be ashamed. At this moment it is, in a manner more dramatic and amazing than the Founding Fathers could have dreamed, the bastion of freedom and the hope of the world.

The point is not affected that democracy everywhere is on trial and is in peril. Its fate and its future depend upon spiritual renewal at a deep level. Such renewal is inconceivable save as an expression of what men have always called religion. No one can prescribe the course or mark the bounds of a fresh creative religious impulse. At this point humility becomes all men—certainly all Christians who are taught to hold in the highest esteem this rare virtue. It is written in one of the greatest Christian books:

> The wind bloweth where it listeth, and thou hearest the sound thereof, but canst not tell whence it cometh, and whither it goeth: so is every one that is born of the Spirit.[1]

At the same time it is most proper and fitting that Christians should bear their witness. There are three very strong

[1] St. John 3:8.

reasons for believing that Christianity will not be superseded religiously but will be the major factor in the spiritual rebirth that must surely come.

FINALITY OF FIGURE OF CHRIST

First, the figure of Christ as we have it in the New Testament represents something so profound, so inclusive, and so appealing that we are bound to regard it as a final thing in religion.

It is strange how many different movements and points of view converge on this thought. The very listing of some of them is extraordinarily strong evidence for the finality of Jesus Christ.

Liberal Protestantism is witness number one. This was a movement originating in Germany in the closing decades of the nineteenth century. Its great theologian was Albrecht Ritschl. He was a disciple of the great Immanuel Kant in his world outlook and in his convictions as to what we know and do not know. Our knowledge, Kant held, as regards the world of things outside us is very limited. What we know is our own sense impressions. They are shaped in large measure by the structure of our minds. But in the realm of values it is another story. Here we are on solid ground. Applying this to religion, Ritschl held that we only know God as revealed in Christ. Christ has the value of God and is all the God we know.

The great popularizer of Ritschlianism and the man who transmitted it to the Anglo-American world was Adolph von Harnack. His book published in translation in 1900 under the title, *What is Christianity?*, is the classical statement of Liberal Protestantism. In many ways it is unorthodox and radical; yet the overshadowing impression the work leaves is that for Harnack Christ is Christianity and is final. Even when he tries to put the weight on the teacher and the teaching, he seems to be transfixed by the power of Christ's Person.

Roman Catholic Modernism arose about the time of Harnack. It was an attempt to combine Newman's theory of development and William James' American pragmatism as a way of vindicating to the modern mind the full Catholic system. The greatest of the Modernists was Father George Tyrrell, whose book *Christianity at the Crossroads* made upon the present writer in his Seminary course an ineffaceable impression. And the thing that stands out in recollection is Tyrrell's sense of the unchangeable Christ even as he is the advocate of development and change.

Tyrrell and his friends were critical of Harnack and were influenced by another German—an Alsatian named Albert Schweitzer. Schweitzer enjoys today an international reputation. Tens of thousands would hail him as the greatest humanitarian of our dark age and as the greatest living human being. It is less well known that Schweitzer started out as a theological professor and was a radical New Testament "critic." He opposed Harnack and the Liberal School with vehemence, presenting Jesus as entirely under the influence of current apocalyptic ideas in His thinking about Himself as Messiah. In the Christ going to His Cross there seems to be, in Schweitzer's view, a considerable element of delusion. Yet he closes his learned and lengthy treatise, *The Quest of the Historical Jesus,* with words that contradict his own scholarship and wing their way straight into the hearts of men.

He comes to us as One unknown, without a name, as of old, by the lake-side, he came to those men who knew him not. He speaks to us the same word: 'Follow thou me!' and sets us to the tasks which he has to fulfill for our time. He commands. And to those who obey him, whether they be wise or simple, he will reveal himself in the toils, the conflicts, the sufferings, which they shall pass through in his fellowship, and, as an ineffable mystery, they shall learn in their own experience who he is.[2]

We are surely not in error when we conclude that it was this unknown yet well know Jesus Christ who sent Albert into the heart of Equatorial Africa to take to ignorant, diseased, fearful black men the healing balm of modern medicine. Nor is it possible we are in error when we repeat in faith the unforgettable word:

Inasmuch as ye did it unto one of the least of these my brethren, ye did it unto me.[3]

Passing over many other witnesses, including Karl Barth and Emil Brunner, who under the stimulus of the first Existentialist proper, Soren Kierkegaard, started after World War I a great revival of Protestant Orthodoxy, we note two very different testimonies. The first is the conclusion of Paul Tillich, one of the seminal minds of our time, and a thinker also of unlimited sophistication, that it is not only possible but inevitable to believe in "the appearance of ultimate reality in a historic person, Jesus Christ. For Christian faith," he continues, "this event is in a profound sense the center of history."[4]

If this message is true, Christian theology has received a foundation which transcends the foundation of any other theology and which

[2] Albert Schweitzer, *The Quest of the Historical Jesus* (New York: The Macmillan Co., 1948).

[3] St. Matthew 25:40.

[4] In *The Christian Answer*, Van Dusen, Ed. (New York, Charles Scribner's Sons), p. 18.

itself can not be transcended. Christian theology has received something which is absolutely concrete and absolutely universal at the same time. No myth, no mystical vision, no metaphysical principle, no sacred law, has the concreteness of a personal life.[5]

Our last witness is one of the most striking of all. He is a German Jewish psychiatrist, Dr. Karl Stern, already quoted, who in a volume as rich in content as it is arresting in title, *The Pillar of Fire,* tells the story of his gradual discovery of "the truth as it is in Jesus" and his eventual conversion to Christianity and the Roman Catholic Church. This conversion is not, as so often with English and American converts, primarily to a Church and Church system, though these are evidently very important to Stern. It is to Christ that he is, in the first instance, converted—to Christ as Messiah, as Saviour, as the God-Man, as the center of history, as the creator of a higher view of man and a deeper understanding of human experience.

Someone once remarked that you should try experimentally to live for one day as if the Gospel were true, even if you do not believe it. In the same way I invite you to think of the nature of Man as if Christ had been God-Man and died for your and my salvation. The whole of anthropology as conceived by philosophers and psychologists is at once deepened in a very peculiar way. It is as if a great, but albeit two-dimensional, picture received a third dimension and came to life. . . .

Christ challenged not only the apparent chaos of history but the meaninglessness of personal existence. . . .

And there was no doubt about it—towards Him we had been running, or from Him we had been running away, but all the time He had been in the center of things.[6]

[5] Paul Tillich, *Systematic Theology* (Chicago: University of Chicago Press), Vol. I, p. 16.

[6] Karl Stern, *Pillar of Fire* (New York, Harcourt, Brace & Company), pp. 228, 229, 302.

DEVELOPMENT POTENTIAL OF CHRISTIANITY

Second, Christianity has shown throughout its history a marvelous power of adaptability and adjustment. Its development potential exceeds that of any other great world religion. At the same time it has shown through all change and growth a persistent unmistakable continuity and identity.

The first grave crisis of Christianity came very early. It was the problem of Gentiles and the Jewish Law. St. Paul, once a Pharisee of the Pharisees, was on hand to deal with this life-and-death issue and to enunciate a profound and lastingly revolutionary doctrine of Christian freedom.

The second severe problem of relationship and adjustment arose when the new Christian religion confronted and was confronted by the religion, philosophy, and psychology of Hellenistic culture. The outcome of this extremely complex situation was three-fold: (a) the historic Catholic Church with its Creed, Scriptures, Ministry, Sacraments, and Liturgical Worship, emerged; (b) Hellenism and Hebraism entered into a marriage of mind and soul through the mediation of the Christian Church; (c) Christianity, which had from the first been persecuted by the Roman authorities, was officially recognized by the State, and Christ the King was elevated above Caesar.

The third crisis of Christianity came with the fall of Rome and the inrush of the barbarians. A second Paul, Augustine of Hippo, was at hand to interpret the ways of God and the hard problems of history. The philosophy of history outlined by the great African in *The City of God* was so satisfying that it paved the way for a new Christian civilization, the Middle Ages, and was unchallenged by the intellect of Europe for more than a millennium.

In the fifteenth and sixteenth centuries a new crisis began with the advent of the Copernican concept of the world and its dethronement of planet earth as the center of the universe. This crisis has continued in many phases. In the nineteenth century the doctrine of evolution required a drastic adaptation on the part of Christian thought. About the same time a new and radically different approach to the Bible and its interpretation won wide acceptance after a period of confusion, fear, and hopeless struggle.

In our century the crisis is on a wider front. All human concerns are involved. Not only Christianity but democracy and Western Civilization are at stake. The heart of the contemporary emergency is the collapse of personal meaning in a life-order dominated by technology and industrialization. This brings us to the third asset of the Christian religion.

DEMOCRACY—A SEGMENT OF CHRISTIAN CONSCIOUSNESS

Third, democracy as a view of man could never have arisen without the preceding Christian ages. It is in fact a segment of Christian consciousness and teaching with respect to the nature and destiny of man. As no concept of man can stand alone in lordly metaphysical independence, defying the universe, democracy is in search of a philosophy and a deeper faith. Where is it so likely to find what it seeks as in the Christian understanding of Reality and in the Christian doctrines of God as Heavenly Father, Jesus Christ as Lord, and all men as brothers?

In the preceding chapter we analyzed the resolution which Christ brought about in man's understanding of himself, God and the world. We tried to recapture the dynamic of love's assault upon the forces of selfishness, malice, and fear. We noted the amazing effect on man's view of his own being.

We surveyed the result in the emergence of a new, unique historical man.

These are the two basic Christian contributions: (a) Jesus Christ as Lord because of the appearance in him as event in history of Absolute Reality, Perfect Love, the Eternal Father; and (b) "the new being in Christ," in Paul Tillich's exciting phrase—man knowing himself as a new creation through the Cross and Resurrection; man freed in Christ from anxiety, despair, guilt, and death; man conscious of himself as a son and heir of Him who is Eternal and Immortal—a joint-heir with the crucified, risen, reigning Lord Christ.

These great occurrences had great consequences, first in man's experience and self-consciousness, and secondly in his activity and accomplishments in history. The first stage is the longest and is primary in the so-called Dark Ages and in the Mediaeval Period. The second stage is manifest as primary with the art, thought, and discoveries of Renaissance man, and continues with some interruptions and reactions but ever increasing momentum down to the present age. The rise of Democratic man, endowed he assumes by nature and nature's God with certain inalienable rights, whether they be with John Locke and George Mason "life, liberty, and property" or with Thomas Jefferson and the *Declaration of Independence* "life, liberty, and the pursuit of happiness," marks the coming to age of the new historical man. This man has been nurtured in the lap of the Christian Church; he has nursed at the breast of the Christian Scriptures; his tutor in the knowledge of Christ and himself has been the Spirit of Truth, proceeding from the Father; but now he has reached the time of independence and self-assertion. He imagines himself to be self-sufficient and able to pursue his own devices without benefit of Divine inspiration or reference to sources of vitality and energy deeper than his individual being.

ART AS MIRROR OF HISTORY

The history of art has been cited by Tillich as affording a series of mirrors for the apprehension of modern man's changing spiritual climate and situation. Art, he believes, is always a more sensitive spiritual barometer than science or philosophy. Four such mirrors (this metaphor is my own) in which historical man is held up to the light, are Giotto's pictures of St. Francis and his monks, the portraits of Titian, Rembrandt's later portraits, and portraits painted since the middle of the nineteenth century.

In the *Francis* of Giotto we are still in the world in which transcendent spiritual powers penetrate and transfigure individual and earthly being. Man is a new creation "in Christ" and in communion with the Source of all being and all life.

In the portraits of Titian we see Renaissance man, man as portrayed psychologically and dramatically by William Shakespeare at the high tide of the "New Birth." Man is now more individuated; he is harmonious and free; he is at once human and divine; in the glory of this consciousness man finds the meaning of existence.

Rembrandt is the artist of a Protestant and Calvinist culture, in which however the center of meaning has unmistakably shifted from the Divine to the human, from the consciousness of God, Heaven, an earth filled with the Divine presence, to isolated, individual self-consciousness. Rembrandt's portraits show us "personalities who are like self-enclosed worlds—strong, lovely, tragic but unbroken, carrying the marks of their unique histories in every line of their faces." They recognize the absolute demands of conscience and hope for the salvation arbitrarily dealt out by a Sovereign, self-detached Deity; but they are not happy and they do not enjoy their freedom.

If, finally, we look at portraits of men of wealth and power in the late nineteenth century, we see man at a still different stage. We see highly marked individuality, developed intellect, and great strength of will. We confront the personality that has created by technical reason the vast, interlocking, all-encompassing structure of capitalistic industrialism. Spiritual creativity has been replaced by technical rationality and ultimate meaning has been lost. Tradition may be honored still, but this personality is shaped by immanent, predominantly material and mechanistic forces. Tillich thinks that in this last stage, characterized by the union of will-power and technical rationality, the way is prepared for the Fascist (and presumably the Communist) type in which all remnants of the classical and humanist as well as the Christian ideal are erased.[7]

TWENTIETH CENTURY AND PRODIGAL SON

The twentieth century has many appearances of being the time on which the ends of the world have come. It is also the era of the Prodigal Son coming to himself. Man knows today his alienation from the sources of his true being. He knows that he has squandered his spiritual inheritance. He knows that the science of which he has been so proud is not enough. He is only too well aware that it has not auto-

[7] See the Essay "The World Situation" in the volume cited above, *The Christian Answer*. The analysis I have attempted is essentially the same as Tillich's, phrased, however, in my own way and not to be attributed in this form to him.

For a parallel use of Michaelangelo and Rubens in relation to the experience of Luther, see my Essay "Spiritual Antecedents" in *Anglican Evangelicalism*, Zabriskie, Ed. (Philadelphia, Church Historical Society), p. 69.

matically brought in the brave new world of humanist dreams and that it could well be the instrument not of salvation but of utter and horrible destruction.

Man knows his need, his precarious condition, his hunger in the midst of plenty. He remembers the existence which was once his in his Father's house, and recalls that

> The sea of faith
> Was once, too, at the full, and round earth's shore
> Lay like the folds of a bright girdle furled.

He wills to return, to find again sanity and peace, to receive once more daily bread for his spirit. He wills this even when he denies the impulse and embarks upon ambitious and grandiose plans for erecting some edifice of material and social salvation.

One cannot doubt that this is true of the Russian masses and many leaders. In time it will be true of the Chinese. It is certainly true of the disillusioned Germans and of sobered Europeans generally. It is true of the long-suffering, greatly enduring British people. There are many signs that it is true, too, of Americans.

Our great Republic has all at once come of age and has with bewildering suddenness come dead against stark, shocking, frightening reality. We know as a people that our problems are grave. We know that our quiet continental safety is no more. Isolation is no more than a dream. Twice we have entered, not by deliberate, clear purpose, but with an inexorable instinctive self-propulsion, wars of world-scale magnitude and have provided the resources and manpower that in each case turned the tide and achieved military victory. We have forged the most terrible weapons in the history of war. We cannot doubt, however, that they are liable sooner or later to be turned against us. We are a peaceful unwarlike people. We hate war and would be done with it, but we are compelled to prepare for battle. And the battles ahead, if they must needs come, will be fought on a scale and with a cold relentlessness that will make all previous war look like a child's game.

This is the fate of man—of American man, of "free" man, of self-sufficient, individual man—in our time. It is a fate we can strive against, try to out-wit, hope to escape by good luck or by God's mercy. But it is not a fate we can change by wishes or fears or the simple exercise of free will or even the motion and the current, too long delayed, of a will to love and understand even the evil and the possessed.

This is the Far Country in which twentieth century man finds himself. From it he can return only if he comes to himself and in humility and repentance wills to reclaim the inheritance of his Father's house. Costing self-knowledge is the first essential. The will to act on this knowledge is the second.

CAN AMERICANS WAKE UP?

Can Americans really awake to the condition and need of man today—including American man? Can they see themselves in the parable of the Prodigal Son who finally "hit bottom" in a far country? We should be able to. We have many advantages. We retain the priceless blessing of freedom, with the opportunity for full discussion and thought. There were never before so many commentators and analysts hired to inform and stimulate or so many opportunities for leaders in national life to reach the people. There was probably never before so developed an appetite for hearing and seeing as that of the American public at this moment.

Another notable advantage, touched on in the last Chapter and discussed at greater length in Chapter II, is the extent and intensity of interest in religion among Americans. This interest is very varied but for the great majority it is along traditional, semi-orthodox, Biblical lines. This situation has special danger, but it may well be the white hope of the survival and future development of democracy in the world. It guarantees on the part of many millions an existing receptivity to the words and ideas of Christianity.

On the other side, America has been sheltered to an amazing degree from adversity and deep suffering. Since the American Civil War, which was the precursor in many respects, of the great World Wars, we have been in a continent and hemisphere of peace. We have never lost a war in our entire history. The bitterness, humiliation, and psychological devastation of defeat are, except in the case of the Old South, outside our experience.

Then there is the extraordinary prosperity of America. We are the Horatio Alger among the nations—the great success story of history. Our forefathers were adventurers and pioneers who struck it rich for themselves and their posterity. In an incredibly short time, as national histories go, the nation which they founded has advanced to heights of wealth and power hitherto undreamed of.

The outstanding feature of the modern period is industrial and technical development. From this standpoint the United States is the characteristic modern nation. It has outpaced the world in developing a technological system and in reaping the fruits of this development. These fruits are not merely national riches, military power based on industrial potential, and a position of world leadership. They are also the highest living standard, the widest distribution of wealth, and the most emphatic psychology of freedom which the world has ever seen.

Not unnaturally the American people are material-minded. They are preoccupied with things, their creation, acquisition, and use. They take for granted as necessities many objects and accessories that the rest of mankind regard as luxuries. They are not in love with poverty or plainness. They view prosperity without shame and, rather like the children of Israel in Biblical times, regard it as a mark of Divine favor.

Again, among all peoples Americans are the most optimistic and expectant. They have the least intuition of limitation, the strongest sense of mastery and scientific control. They are congenitally hopeful. Russia is a partial exception, for the Soviet leaders as orthodox Marxists presumably believe that there is no barrier to perfect control over society and nature. The Russian people, however, remain Orientals; their outlook for centuries has been submissive, supine and fatalistic. Such a psychology cannot be changed overnight.

Then the American people are the most imbued with the democratic idea. The Declaration is the *magna carta* of modern democracy. In ringing words it asserted one hundred seventy-five years ago that every individual has as natural, inalienable, God-given rights, life, liberty, and the pursuit of happiness. From the beginning American social, economic, and political life has been founded on this idea. Americans have not only believed it; they have taken it for granted. It has been like the air they breathed. They believe deeply—not to be arbitrary or different but because of experience, facts, and ingrained habit of mind—that freedom has had a lot to do with their success. It will be very difficult to persuade them otherwise.

HUMILITY AND RECOVERY

None of these things makes for humility, which in the Christian scheme is the opposite of the deadly sin of pride and the foundation of all true virtue. St. Paul defined humility when he counseled the Christians of Rome, "every man that is among you, not to think of himself more highly than he ought to think; but to think soberly."[8] He had the same quality in mind, together with the ease of losing it, when he wrote the vain and puffed up members of the Church at Corinth: "Wherefore let him that thinketh he standeth take heed lest he fall."[9] He did not mean self-depreciation. Humility is not that. It is not littleness or meanness in any way. It is the ability and willingness to get outside oneself and to look steadily and clearly at what one sees. It is psychological realism.

Can America learn humility? Can our people see themselves and their possessions and achievements and way of life with some detachment and sense of proportion? Can they be realistic about the American way, its values, defects, and prospects in the world in which we live? Are they able to recognize themselves along with Englishmen, Frenchmen, Germans, Russians, Spaniards, Indians, Chinese and all men in the portrait of the Prodigal Son drawn by Jesus Christ in the story that ever since has been called by this name?

If Americans can do this—if they can be awakened to the real plight and real need of man in our day and their own involvement and responsibility in the wounds of our reeling, "possessed" twentieth century world—, there is hope of recovery, of reconciliation, of health and new life. If we remain

[8] Romans 12:3.
[9] I Corinthians 10:12.

self-absorbed, insular, parochial, unimaginative, blind, Pharisaical, the outlook at least to human eyes is very dark. The one shaft of light that now pierces the growing dusk of the proud modern gods, vanishes. Gloom alone is left. Freedom passes, and mankind puts on again the chains of slavery.

This is the meaning of the crisis of our day. This is the decision that mankind is forced to make. A new day of the Lord is at hand. It is as it was in the time of Joel the prophet:

Put ye in the sickle, for the harvest is ripe: come, get you down; for the press is full, the fats overflow; for their wickedness is great.

Multitudes, multitudes in the valley of decision: for the day of the Lord is near in the valley of decision.

The sun and the moon shall be darkened, and the stars shall withdraw their shining.

The Lord also shall roar out of Zion, and utter his voice from Jerusalem; and the heavens and the earth shall shake: but the Lord will be the hope of his people, and the strength of the children of Israel.[10]

Let us, in preparation for this day and in the spirit of a great hope, take our American way and hold it up to the mirror of Jesus Christ, the image of God. Let us do so in the boldness of humility, nothing flinching; for we know that no such act is ever without its Divine reward.

What Is the American Way?

By this phrase "the American way" we mean, first of all, the way of freedom for the individual as he lives, works, and seeks happiness. We mean the absence of coercion, duress, regimentation. We mean the preservation to every individual of basic human rights. This is a part of the definition of

[10] Joel 3:13-16.

democracy, and the American way, all would agree, includes as central the democratic way and the democratic idea.

We mean also the fullest possible approach to equality of opportunity. Every individual is born equal and considered equal so far as anything external and arbitrary is concerned. The state will not catalogue him or dictate to him his job or in any way interfere with him save for reasons of urgent necessity—the safety and defence of the state and the preservation to the greatest possible extent of the liberty and equality of all citizens. Furthermore, it is implicit in the meaning of the American way that social structures and traditions are elastic rather than rigid, with a view again to safeguarding freedom and equality, and that anything approaching a caste system is rejected.

The second component element in the meaning of "the American way" is brotherhood. This is the American way of saying it. In France one speaks of fraternity. Our closest approach to this sense of the latter word is in the phrases "fraternal orders" and "Greek Letter Fraternities." It is notable, however, that we always say "fraternity brother."

The French Revolution was less individual-centered in its ideological bent and phraseology than the earlier, English-inspired American Revolution. To "liberty and equality" the ardent, more glowing Gallic spirit added "fraternity." The influence of Rousseau was partly responsible for this. He worked on original lines, more or less, and was not strictly a Liberal. His stress was on love, relationship, community, the whole. As we said in an earlier chapter, Rousseau naturalized the Christian "redeemed" man. He secularized the conception of "grace."

Even so American democracy has developed with a very strong orientation to brotherhood, brotherly love, fellowship, easy friendliness. A striking testimony to the truth of this assertion is the observation of the venerable and progressively less "gloomy" Dean Inge, now approaching his ninetieth year, that "of the windy French triad, the English have chosen Liberty, the French Equality, and the Americans Fraternity." The Englishman, he adds, not only lives on an island, he prefers to be one himself. The Frenchman says, my master is my enemy. The Americans like a good mixer.

The Americans do more than this. They believe that all men are brothers. They feel an obligation to practice brotherhood, regardless of race, class, or creed. They think men and nations should be good neighbors, both in cases of need as with the Good Samaritan and in the sense of interest and friendliness. A symbol of this side of America is the nearly universal practice (except in crowded cities) of having open front lawns, commonly without fences. The American way is the way of brotherhood.

Thirdly, the phrase "the American way" has a material connotation. It carries for those who use it the force of progress, prosperity, high living standards, constant material improvement. It suggests more and better bathrooms, an overwhelming majority of all the telephones and automobiles in the world, supremacy in the production and distribution of radios and television sets, continual advance in inventions, machines, gadgets, automatic contrivances, conveniences and comforts of every kind. It also implies free enterprise, efficient organization, keen competition, aggressive advertising, strong labor unions, the value in everything of business sense and keeping up to date. It is synonymous with push and practicality.

A symbol of this element is the fact that the only native American philosophy is pragmatism or the general doctrine that truth is what works. William James is commonly regarded as the most characteristic American philosopher. His only competitor would be John Dewey. A one-time colleague and friend of James at Harvard, George Santayana, himself a fascinating cross between a New England Puritan mother and a Spanish father in whom, however, the Puritan and American strain failed to take, once said of James that his incursions into the domain of philosophy were of the nature of raids.

So we may summarize and interpret the American way. It has never been and could not be precisely defined. Individual attempts at expounding the meaning of a very widely used phrase of our common speech, would doubtless differ considerably. Nearly every one, however, would agree on the three statements that it is a democratic way; it is a brotherly, friendly way; and it is a way of material and practical emphasis.

Over against this way of a nation and people, let us look at Jesus Christ. It seems entirely natural to do so. Somehow we suppose He was a great exemplar of democracy. We connect Him directly with the American way. We may suppose that this way is the Christian way. "The Way" is one of the earliest designations of Christianity.[11] There are even those who think, without really thinking, that Christianity is the American way in an abstract form.

DANGER OF SHALLOWNESS

The story is told of an American businessman who was a delegate to the Oxford Conference on *Church, Community, and State* in the summer of 1937. The conference was broken down into sections for discussion and study. In every section

[11] Acts 19:9, 23.

were to be found some of the ablest theologians and keenest intellects in Christendom. They often differed sharply with each other, and they nearly all gave the impression that to find the Christian position on anything was exceedingly difficult. The American listened to this go on day after day. Finally his impatience was too great to be contained any longer. He arose and said, "I don't see why every one seems to think the Sermon on the Mount is so difficult. I follow it all the time."

There was justification for this man's impatience. There were a large number of subtle intellects floating around at Oxford. There were many superfine distinctions made. There was much theological buck-passing. The Europeans tended to be pessimistic, and there was a disposition to explain present difficulties by reference to past mistakes. Just after the Conference when I had the great privilege of visiting at Bishopthorpe outside York the great Archbishop William Temple, he told me with keen relish of a remark he had got off at Oxford: "The modern substitute for garnishing the tombs of the prophets is confessing the sins of one's fore-fathers."

So our fellow-countryman had a point and deserved sympathy. Yet his remark about the Sermon on the Mount was shallow and unworthy. No one this side of the kingdom of the angels has ever followed fully and always the great Sermon. It is the pre-eminent statement of Christ's royal law of love, by which constantly we are judged and brought to our knees in penitence and shame. No better example could be given of the special peril that besets the life, thought, and spirituality of America, namely, complacent superficiality. A material, sensate culture inevitably tends to accent surfaces and dry up the depths. There is the utmost danger that all things will become two-dimensional, like the motion pictures of America which have flooded the markets of the world and have conveyed to all other nations so distorted a rendition of the unending sensationalism of life in the United States.

A FRESH EVALUATION

At the same time there is much that is great and lasting in the American tradition and the American accomplishment. We do not need to be apologetic, inferior, defensive. We do need and should make now a fresh, informed, realistic evaluation of Americanism. We need to see what it is, where it has come from, where it is now, and where it is going.

This can be made only if we desire to know the truth, only if we believe in seeing *the things that are as they are.* Truth, said Alfred North Whitehead, is the conformation of appearance to reality. We might add that it is the will to resist and surmount the deceptiveness of specious appearances. Such a disposition and enterprise are not easy. It is often pleasanter and it seems safer to linger in the shallows. But the rushing stream is there and must be crossed. So though truth is never comfortable and requires of its practitioners courage and energy, it is in the end the only final comfort and the only possible security. In this connection there is a wonderful saying of St. Paul, tucked in inconspicuously at the very end of his Corinthian Epistles. "For we can do nothing against the truth, but for the truth."

This was the point of view of Jesus Christ, set forth in two remarkable statements written in the Gospel according to St. John. "Ye shall know the truth and the truth shall make you free." "I am the way, the truth, and the life." The first of these sayings has tended in the Liberal period to hold

and increase its popularity. The second has remained meaningful, as it is in all cases bound to, for the faithful Christian.
For the modern, emancipated, liberated, rationalistic, scientific, humanist mind it has become a *scandalon*, a scandal,
a stumbling block, a stone of intellectual offense. Yet the
two belong together. The first cannot be understood as it was
originally meant and as Christianity has always understood
it without the second.

Thomas Jefferson, who has been called, on the one hand,
the last man of the Renaissance and, on the other, the first
Liberal, was enamored of the first of our two sayings of
Jesus Christ. It expressed his faith and hope, and he caused
it to be made the motto of the great university which he
founded, the University of Virginia. In adopting it as his
favorite saying the Sage of Monticello stripped it of its context and not a few of his successors and fellow-countrymen
have done the same ever since.

In the *Declaration of Independence* there is something of
the same tendency, not with respect to this saying specifically,
but in the quite parallel and closely related doctrine of absolute natural law. This doctrine underlies the reasoning
and appeal to reason of the *Declaration*. It is the basis of
the assertion as self-evident truths (a mathematical phrase)
"that all men are created equal; that they are endowed by
their Creator with certain inalienable rights; that among
these are life, liberty, and the pursuit of happiness."

Unconsciously there is visible here, from our present position where we cannot help seeing so much else that has happened, a move away from Christian Theism, with its central
concept of a living God who is present in his continuously
re-created creation, who in the fulness of time personally enters into history in the form of a servant as a human being,

and who by his forthgoing Divine Spirit is the never abdicating Director of the immense, terrible, sublime, symphonic drama of time and history. Instead of this we have in Jefferson the Deism of the eighteenth century, according to which God at some point called into being and set in motion a marvelous physical and mathematical mechanism, the world, which is as rational through and through as the physics of Newton and which operates by means of inherent immutable laws. It is evident that such a conception stands midway between the Christian conception of creation and the absolutely self-sufficient, strictly God-less world of Karl Marx and Dialectical Materialism. It is striking also that the classical *laissez faire* doctrine of economic law, which Marx regarded it as his life-work to complete and draw out to its logical conclusion, is based not upon Christian or even Greek thought but upon this same deistic, mathematical, radically rationalistic conception of reality. In this scheme God is not the transcendent author of law, but is identified by implication with immutable truth able to be grasped fully and certainly in all areas by the human mind. The divorce of Christ as the truth from independent eternal truth follows logically and inevitably.

CHRIST AND THE AMERICAN WAY

If this whole development was exaggerated and bound to lead to disastrous confusion—if Christian Theism is much sounder, more whole, more balanced, more in accordance with experience and facts—if Jesus Christ was and is the truth, then we must return to Him. We must look at Him and hold up to Him as to a clear, undistorting but also unflattering mirror all our ways. We must hear what He has to say to America today—at this moment of critical testing and high destiny when mankind has reached a great double crossroads of history and must take one turning or the other.

There are many approaches which might be made to this all-important question of Jesus Christ and the American way. We shall take the one suggested by the foremost of our state papers—the foundation document on which the nation and the liberties and privileges of all her citizens are based, and which on July Fourth last was one hundred seventy-five years old. We shall take the phrase "life, liberty, and the pursuit of happiness" and seek for a short concluding space to hear what Jesus Christ has to say respecting these realities. Since the whole development of man and history out of which the doctrine of basic natural rights came, was the offspring and issue of Christianity, *we can assume that there is no question of contradiction as between democracy and Christ.* What we shall expect to find is *a relationship of enlarged and deepened affirmation as between the truths of the Declaration and the perspective of the mind of One who came as "the way, the truth, and the life."*

(1) LIFE

Jesus Christ is the Apostle of life. There is no word more often on His lips, no thought more central in His teaching, no determination more motivating in the immortal deed of death by which He brought to a world salvation. Two sentences from St. John sum this up, as so often, in a final way. "I am come that they might have life, and that they might have it more abundantly."[12] "For God sent not his Son into the world to condemn the world: but that the world through him might be saved."[13]

[12] St. John 10:10.
[13] St. John 3:17.

But Jesus has the most searching and profound things to say as to what life is. It is, He warns, not meat and drink, not dress and fashion, not comfort and luxury, not wealth or vast possessions. It is not anything material or sensuous at all. It is a quality of mind and heart. It is an attribute of the spirit within a man.

Jesus does not mean that matter can be treated as unimportant, that bread is unessential, that the body is to be despised and neglected. On the contrary, Jesus is unique among the great spiritual leaders and religious founders of the ancient world in His acceptance of matter, bread, the body, the beauty of nature, love and friendship among men. He is emphatically not an idealist (in the philosophical sense), not a mentalist, not an ascetic, not a Manichean. He is uninfected by the vain spiritual dream of life lived "as in a bodiless condition." He puts "daily bread" at the center of prayer. At the end of His life by His own solemn act and institution He associated with His death and life to be, bread and wine, making them forever the central sacrament of His eternal presence and power. Christianity is not, and can never be except by wrenching distortion, an anti-material religion. It is the religion of creation, of God as the great artist, architect, fashioner, and engineer of matter. "In the beginning God created. . . . And God saw everything that he had made, and, behold, it was very good."[14] For this reason it was the mother out of whose womb came science and technology. For the same reason it is the one religion which has the resources to meet and master, but not reject, the materialistic drive of our urgent, restless age.

Yet there is no compromise with materialism, theoretical

[14] Genesis 1:1, 31.

or practical. God is, and "is a Spirit."[15] Man is created in the image of God and is called to the imitation of the Heavenly Father, whose perfection is His love and generosity.[16] Man as a spirit lives by the Word or self-communicating will and faculty of God. "Man," said Jesus Christ to the Tempter in the Wilderness, "shall not live by bread alone, but by every word that proceeds from the mouth of God."[17] This is Christianity's word against Marx and Marxist Communism. But there is a word that democratic capitalism, most notably exemplified in the United States, needs to ponder—that is against the greed, corruption, practical materialism, and obsession with things which are rampant in our society and in which we are all spiritually involved. It is the word: "Take heed, and beware of all covetousness; for a man's life does not consist in the abundance of his possessions."[18]

What, then, is life? In what does it consist? It consists, first of all and above all, in being "rich toward God."[19] By this is meant, as the immediate context and Christ's teachings as a whole together clearly show, animation in the whole range of one's being, not by the spirit of self-love and self-service but by the Spirit of God. The meaning of such animation is shown concretely in the Beatitudes[20] of the Sermon on the Mount and more generally in Christ's Summary of the Law[21] (the most wonderful example on record of living by every word of God, for it is the selection and connection of two widely separated Old Testament sayings)

[15] St. John 4:24.
[16] St. Matthew 5:45-48.
[17] *Ibid*, 4:4, RSV.
[18] St. Luke 12:15, RSV.
[19] *Ibid*, 12:21.
[20] St. Matthew 5:3-11.
[21] St. Mark 12:29-31. cf. Deut. 6:4 and Leviticus 19:18.

as love of God and love of neighbor, and in the Golden Rule.[22] The result of such animation is newness of life and character; it is faith, hope, integrity, integration, a sense of reality and purpose, joy, and peace.

These conceptions and impulsions were the theme of Christ's teaching during His life. They gained, however, a new access of power and meaning through His death and resurrection seen by the eyes of faith and understood as the Word and Act of God Himself. Here the apostolic writings of the Church must be studied and taken as seriously as the Gospels. The thing that is certain is that in the most remarkable way those who believed and entered the Christian Society experienced a sense of new being in Christ.

This was and is the Christian revolution. It is the end of all other revolution, which without it is twisted and turned into blacker reaction, and the last state is worse than the first. Man in America and everywhere has before him today the choice of mere living or of new being in Christ.

(2) LIBERTY

Christianity from the beginning has meant spiritual liberty. This was the result of the new creation in Christ; it was the extension in sense of release and freedom of the new life which He brought. There is nothing in the New Testament more thrilling than the way in which St. Paul speaks of Christian freedom and contends for it against all who would bind man by spiritual legalism. It is as if one could feel still the fresh, clean wind of the Spirit of God blowing through and cleansing the minds of men. "For freedom did Christ set us free: stand fast therefore, and be not entangled again in a yoke of bondage."[23]

---

[22] St. Luke 6:31; St. Matthew 7:12.
[23] Galatians 5:1, ASV.

This was in no direct sense a political doctrine. It was compatible in Paul's own mind with submission to the civil authority of the Roman Empire, for he specifically counsels such submission. When he writes a Christian master on behalf of a runaway slave, he writes of Christian charity and brotherhood, even of equality in Christ, but he does not reproach the master for owning slaves. One factor here is Christian *other-worldliness* based on the mistaken belief that history had but a short time to go. Then would come the return of Christ and the end of the present world-order. It is very important to keep this whole complex of facts in mind and to note, in comparing the primitive Christian period with modern Communism, as not a few including the late Professor Harold Laski have done, the sharp contrast here with contemporary *this-worldliness*. Communism is the first universal salvation religion to be absolutely *this-worldly*, though Confucianism and Judaism approach this. The question with each of them is whether we have to do with a really universal religion.

Yet in the end Christianity was on the side of liberty in every sphere and for all life. It was in a Christian civilization that democracy arose and slavery was overthrown. The sequence here is notable, for though no Christian nation had ever countenanced slavery in its own borders prior to the introduction of African blacks into the American colonies, the Church had been and remained slow about any absolute condemnation of the institution as such. Democracy, the rise of all citizens to freedom and self-government, was followed by the overthrow of slavery. In Greece and Rome this did not occur, even though in the case of Rome there was in Stoic ideology a doctrine of the natural equality and brotherhood of all men. The conclusion is evident: the root of modern democracy is new and different; it is Christianity.

Christianity believes in freedom because it is the breath of the Christian life. It is the meaning of the life and death of Christ. Also Christianity believes in man's creation in the Divine image. It believes in the spirithood and essential immateriality of man, even though the spirit of man arises in relation to a physical organism and this is a fixed and unalterable relationship in our present time-space order. This means that man has a natural freedom and power of choice. He is not a thing, not an animal, but a spiritual being with "power on his own act and on the world." This is of God's ordination. He Himself respects this freedom which He has given man. He gives man large elbow room in his historical existence. This strategy of Divine persuasion, based evidently on the highest valuation of freedom, can only be partial in the created order. In this order there must be boundaries and laws, else chaos and destruction would ensue. When it comes, however, to redeeming man, to saving him from himself, to winning him to free cooperation with the purpose of God in creation, we see in a new and marvelous way the height and depth of the Divine valuation of freedom. God will use no force, no coercion, no psychological compulsion, no fanfare of propaganda and mass persuasion, to win His child, man. In the fulness of time He comes—but in the form of a slave, as a man of the people, a carpenter and a countryman. And He comes to let Himself be killed—to die as a criminal, the victim of Jewish idealism and Roman justice. This act was the redemption of the world by Almighty God. It occurred in an obscure province of the Roman Empire under an obscure colonial governor. And even afterward God made no move to coerce or compel. He left man still free, to accept the love of Christ or to reject

Him. Redemption even more than Creation and Providence must respect the freedom of man.

FINALITY OF DEMOCRACY

What does this mean for politics and society? It means that freedom must be the basic form of life. *This is the Divine intention. Democracy is right at this point and represents a final political and governmental development.* It is possible and needful to perfect democracy, for it is human and weak, never a finished achievement. But it cannot be superseded. It is as final as individuality and self-consciousness in the creation of man.

What of freedom in the economic sphere? This is a critical hot-spot in our present world. Three positions are maintained. One is Totalitarianism, the system of Russia as it was of Hitler's Germany, in which freedom is simply annulled, cancelled out with a stroke of the pen or nod of the head; and man is returned at one bound to the ancient pre-Christian and pre-Greek condition of absolutistic statism, with no rights as such at all.

A second position is British Socialism. It arose democratically and is valiantly committed to the goal of maintaining the essential liberties in a framework of state ownership of the means of production and state administration of most public services and national cultural agencies. Whether it will be able to maintain itself as a thoroughly intermediate position, combining full dress Socialism economically and socially with political democracy, is a great unsolved question which only the future can settle. It is clear, however, that the pressure toward Totalitarianism will become much stronger than it is at present.

A MIXED POLITICAL ECONOMY

The third position is that of American democratic Capitalism. In this system there is a general framework of freedom, in the economic as in other spheres. There is freedom for the individual, freedom for enterprise, and the maintenance of democratic government in terms of the opportunity of all to decide who shall govern and what broad policy shall be. But alongside that general structure and basic form of freedom, there have developed many state controls, which will undoubtedly continue.

The American system, as now developed, is a mixed political economy and I believe we all need as Americans, and perhaps especially as Christian Americans, to strengthen our grasp of this idea of a mixed or pluralistic society. It is the hope of the world in the face of the terrific drive of the age toward a monistic or monolithic state-society. The mixed economy of the United States as presently developed has at least five distinct factors. The first is free enterprise. This remains the essential form of American society and the mainspring of industry, business, and professional life. The second factor is state controls such as taxation, credit-management, and the outlawry of monopoly. The third factor is organized labor and its enormous power exerted through collective bargaining. This power is so great that it is now following capital in being placed under state controls. The fourth factor is voluntary cooperative ventures, of which the kinds are legion and the possibilities endless. This, however, is so far the least important of the five. The fifth and last factor is limited governmental agencies for strengthening the business economy or the public interest at emergency points, including social security.

There are many Americans who feel, some with deep bitterness, that these various qualifications of earlier "pure" freedom of enterprise have weakened and even ruined America. They believe that the cause of democracy is now sore beset even "in the land of the free and the home of the brave." They think that the camel's nose is already in the Washington tent, and that Socialist intrusion will from here on out increase "in greater volume."

No one can say about this with any certainty. The times are too unsure, the possible pressure of outside events too unpredictable. But the most optimistic prospect on the present horizon is a protracted cold war, with America armed to the teeth and her economy forced to shoulder a staggering additional load for many a year. In view of this the discussion even of reversion to simpler liberal ways would be academic. Would it not be more profitable to concentrate positively on the meaning of the American experiment and on the infinite possibilities of the future if we as a people will keep alive the flame of liberty and will steadfastly hold to freedom as the basic determinative form of society irrespective of adjustments and qualifications dictated by necessity? We would do well instead of lamenting the limitations of economic freedom that have come, to rejoice and be glad for the resourcefulness and restraint that have kept us a democracy through the first half of the totalitarian century and have kept our system expanding when by all the orthodox laws from which Marxist calculations have been so industriously and piously drawn, it should have been rent asunder by its own inner contradictions.

This thought is occasion surely for a *Te Deum* in every Cathedral and every Church in America.

Freedom Under God

There is, however, grave danger that we shall be overcome by inward and spiritual contradictions. This is the real peril of the country. This is the warning that Jesus Christ gives us as looking at Him we look also steadily at the American way.

The foundations of freedom are spiritual. It was so in the past. Christian freedom was a thousand six hundred years old before it brought forth the fruit of political, economic, and social democracy. "First the blade, then the ear, then the full corn in the ear."[24] As in the past, so it is now and will be in the future.

There is only one way in which the full corn of freedom as we are blessed with it now in this nation can remain for our enjoyment and that of future generations. It is by repairing the breaches in the foundations. It is by renewal in faith, in dedication to a purpose greater than self, in the vision of the love and glory of God.

"The vision of God," said a great Christian named Irenaeus or "Peaceable One" in the second century—"The vision of God is the life of man." Abraham Lincoln had the same thought when he wrote into his first and original draft of the Gettysburg Address the words "under God."

That we here highly resolve that these dead shall not have died in vain—that this nation, *under God*, shall have a new birth of freedom.

(3) The Pursuit of Happiness

The goal of all human action is happiness. Aristotle based his Ethics on this axiom.

[24] St. Mark 4:28, RV.

Now we call that which is in itself worthy of pursuit more final than that which is worthy of pursuit for the sake of something else. . . .

Now such a thing happiness, above all else, is held to be; for this we choose always for itself and never for the sake of something else.

In these words, among the most influential ever penned, we have, I believe, the ultimate source of the phraseology adopted by Jefferson as the third inalienable natural right of man.

LOVE AND HAPPINESS

Christianity has no quarrel with the pursuit of happiness. If it did, it would be like railing at the law of gravitation or the fact of motion. The greatest theological authority of the Roman Catholic Church, St. Thomas Aquinas, summed up this first law of psychological motion in a succinct phrase. "Happiness," he said, "is the end of human acts." Jesus Christ began, not by questioning but by assuming happiness as the first law of human endeavor. This is why he appeals constantly to desire, to the will to live, even to the idea of reward and punishment: or would it be more accurate to say, blessing and its opposite consequence—misery. In the Beatitudes, for example, He begins each statement of the laws of value in the Kingdom of Heaven with the word *Makarios* in Greek, commonly translated "Blessed." Moffatt, however, translates "Happy," and Weymouth in a note says "Or Happy." The word means literally "to be an object of congratulation," "to be envied."

This is a characteristic note in the outlook and teaching of Jesus. He is interested, as all men are, in life, in liberty, in happiness; but He is interested in each case in the real thing. He penetrates below the surface, cuts underneath prevailing superficial impressions, digs down to the pure vein of the truly real.

As to happiness, which Jesus assumes all men desire and are in some sense pursuing, His point of view is trenchant and clear. It is that simply running here and there after pleasure, or rushing over the surface of life irresponsibly, like a butterfly in the sunlight chasing it knows not what, will not bring happiness. It will stab it to death and bring instead wretchedness. True happiness, says Jesus, comes, and can only come, from acceptance and from giving of self. "Happy are the poor in spirit, for theirs is the kingdom of heaven." "Happy are the meek, for they shall inherit the earth." It was John Milton who spoke of "the magnificent might of meekness" and in his great Ode *Lycidas*, written in memory of a friend who had drowned, thought of him as hearing now

> . . . the unexpressive nuptial song,
> In the blest kingdoms meek of joy and love.

"Happy are the merciful . . . the pure in heart . . . the peacemakers." And, finally, in the saying preserved by St. Paul: "More to be envied is the one who gives, than the one who receives."[25]

All these are statements of the law of love, which for Jesus is the final and absolute reality. It means acceptance, simplicity, submissiveness, surrender—as natural love does, at least transitorily; and it means self-giving, self-denial, sacrifice, the projection of self into the very position of another, for which modern psychology has called out of the Greek language a new and very strong word, *empathy*.

[25] Acts 20:35—Usually translated: "It is more blessed to give than to receive."

Only if you love, and love with something of the royal generosity of God will you be happy. Happiness depends on love, and love is the giving of self to another.

This is the very heart of Jesus' teaching. He put it all in a word of magnificent paradox: "Whosoever shall seek to save his life shall lose it; and whosoever shall lose his life shall preserve it."[26] This His own teaching took Jesus Christ to the Cross. It also made Him the Saviour of the world, the giver of new life to mankind. The Cross means that love is the final truth.

THE CROSS—THE INNER MEANING OF HISTORY

What does all this have to do with America and the American way? It has everything to do with America, with American democracy, with the present crisis of mankind, with the issue—before the whole world at this moment in the starkest sense—of Death or Life. It is the key to the inner meaning of modern history. It is the explanation of the rise of Antichrist in a new guise—as the totalitarian religion of the man-god. It illuminates also the inner peril that besets the American way. This peril is the undermining of the spiritual foundations of democracy by the practical, unadmitted, but real denial of the Cross of Christ and the Law of Love.

This happened in Germany openly and with a flagrant brazenness. The crooked cross of the swastika was the symbol of a defiant rejection of Christ and Christianity. In Russia it has happened also but the world and especially the Protestant Church-world has been slow to believe. This is because Communism is a word stolen from the Christian vocabulary. Not only this. It was presented also as a coming

[26] St. Luke 17:33.

event, scientifically predictable, in which the age-old human dream of equality, justice, love, and lasting peace would be realized. Could such a system be really bad? Is it not perhaps what Christians have always looked for?

The answer has come in terror and confusion. It has come in the revelation of a totalitarian dictatorship more cold, more absolutistic, more hypocritical, more brutal, more repressive, more unconditionally demonic, more irrevocable, more successful in aggression, more dark and threatening than anything the world has known before. All this was predicted more than a hundred years ago by a great English Christian and theologian, Frederick Dennison Maurice. Unlike some remarkable prophecies of a similar type,[27] Maurice's prophecy is not merely detached and *about* others. It speaks also *to* us—it suggests our involvement with mankind and our spiritual crisis. It brings before us, in a manner strikingly contemporaneous, Christ as the central issue and the only Saviour.

. . . If then there be an idea of a universal Prince in men's minds, they will either continue to believe that this idea has been realized in Jesus of Nazareth, or they will seek a realization of it in some other person. And thus we arrive at the third answer which was made to the proclamation of the Creed in the first ages, and which has been made so often since: "This crucified man is not the perfect Being we look for; we want a warrior, a philosopher, a poet, possessing qualities altogether different from those which are brought out in the Gospel narrative, though we may acknowledge that these too have a certain value of their own." Such has for twelve centuries been the belief of a large portion of the world which was once Christian. Another portion of it has declared that they see in the Cross the symbol of love triumphing through suffering, in the Crescent only of power claiming dominion over weakness; that the

[27] Compare p. 171: "Three Remarkable Prophecies."

first is a bond of mutual fellowship among the members of a suffering race; the other the pledge of a universal slavery. That the spirit of the Cross prevails very little in the nations which still profess to honour it; that self-sacrifice is very generally and very systematically denied to be the law of our being,—most of us are ready with shame to confess. And therefore the expectation is surely very reasonable, that the experiment which was so successful in the nations of the East, will be made, under other conditions, in the West. We have had many preparatory Antichrists, many sovereigns reigning by the strength of mind and will, and scorning all other right; why should we doubt that *this* image will be yet more completely manifested?

May God preserve those who live in the day when it is manifested to the world, and when the world goes wandering after it! In that day when intellect and will shall be utterly crushed under the car of the idol which they have set up; in that day when the poor man shall cry, and there shall be no helper, may God teach his saints to proclaim these words to the sons of men: *He was born of the Virgin; He suffered under Pontius Pilate; He was crucified, dead, and buried, and went down into hell; He rose again on the third day; He ascended on high; He sitteth on the right hand of God; He shall come to judge the quick and the dead.* May they be enabled to say, *This is our God; we have waited for him.*[28]

---

[28] *The Kingdom of Christ* (1842), Part II, Chap. IV.

V.

Communism and Christ

And we have known and believed the love that God hath to us. God is
love; and he that dwelleth in love dwelleth in God, and God in him.
—*I John 4:16.*
Christianity is the most avowedly materialist of all the great religions.
—*William Temple of York and Canterbury.*

IN THE END everything depends upon what we think
of as ultimately real. The Doctors of the Middle Ages
were fond of a phrase which means just this. They were
always speaking of the *summa res*—the supreme reality.
This name they gave to God. To them it was a synonym for
Divinity.

This remains everlastingly true. Whatever we believe in
and accept as the ultimately real is our god. It is inevitable
that we shall, in some degree, worship it, and it is certain
that our lives will be affected by our worship. We become
like that which we worship, and we worship what we believe in as ultimate and supreme.

THREE EXAMPLES OF RELIGION

History is full of examples. The Greeks believed in mind
as supreme. They worshipped an intellectual god. Aristotle
in his *Metaphysics* gives a glowing and worshipful description of this deity. He portrays him as an eternal thinker,
absorbed in contemplation everlastingly and to the exclusion
of every other interest or activity. The result is writ large
in the history of Greece and of all later culture.

At the opposite extreme is Islam, a religion based on the idea of arbitrary personal power as ultimate. Such a faith and the worship inseparable from it gave rise inevitably to an ethic of violence and sensuality and issued in the most powerful religious imperialism known prior to the twentieth century.

Still another example, representing quite a different intuition of the Supreme Real, is Hinduism. For the sages of India the Real cannot be less finally than the All—the Being that cannot be qualified—the void or Abyss in which all is included and at the same time stripped of individual color or distinction. The impact of this faith and worship is brilliantly illustrated by the American Brahmin, Ralph Waldo Emerson, who found even the liberality of Unitarianism too confining and rejected Christ for Man, God for Nature. His poem *Brahma* is also a transcript of personal experience. Few poems surely have succeeded in capturing in so short a space such amplitude of thought.

> If the red slayer think he slays,
>   Or if the slain think he is slain,
> They know not well the subtle ways
>   I keep, and pass, and turn again.
>
> Far or forgot to me is near;
>   Shadow and sunlight are the same;
> The vanished gods to me appear;
>   And one to me are shame and fame.
>
> They reckon ill who leave me out;
>   When me they fly, I am the wings;
> I am the doubter and the doubt,
>   And I the hymn the Brahmin sings.

The strong gods pine for my abode,
  And pine in vain the sacred Seven;
But thou, meek lover of the good!
  Find me, and turn thy back on heaven.

If from poetry and philosophical experience we turn to history and culture, we need only gaze at India herself. The bewildering variety of fundamental elements in Hindu culture, the incredible scope of contrasts in mode of worship and way of life within a single tradition, the sense of a magnifying of space at the expense of time which one has in trying to grasp India as a whole—all these clearly reflect the characteristic Hindu intuition of the Ultimate and the Final.

The Example of Communism

No less striking is the example of the newest of the universal salvation religions—Marxist Communism.

The idea that Communism is to be understood as a religious system, with an essentially religious appeal and a religious psychology, is not new. It is not original. It is, however, sufficiently unfamiliar to large numbers of people to make it worthwhile to dwell for a moment on the point.

In 1932 a brilliant if neurotic Englishman, J. Middleton Murry, brought out a book entitled, in imitation of the youthful Shelley, *The Necessity of Communism*. In this book the sentence occurs: ". . . Communism is the one living religion in the Western world today." The late Harold Laski was accustomed from about this same time to emphasize the parallel between modern Communism, with its dynamic faith and expansive, missionary force, and primitive Christianity, with its extraordinary success in out-distancing innumerable rivals and overpowering in less than three centuries the organized police power of the Imperial Roman State.

THE OCTOBER CLUB AT OXFORD

It was in the following year 1933 that a famous debate took place in the Oxford (University) Union on the question: "Resolved, that never again will we fight for king and country." When the House divided and the vote was taken, it was found that the young men of Oxford had decided by a large majority never again to take up arms in defense of their king and country. This news came as a tremendous shock not only to the proud realm immediately concerned but to the whole world.

To the writer, however, the news of the Union debate was far from a surprise. I was in Oxford until December, 1932, and by a series of accidents was given some insight into the founding in October, 1932, of the October Club of the University—a Communist organization for undergraduates. The real character of the new Club was, at first, kept under cover and sometime in October or very early November a Peace Meeting was organized by its leaders and was given wide publicity. The Provost of Oriel, a renowned Aristotelian scholar later knighted and a typical Liberal of the Sir John Simon variety, agreed to take the chair. As the meeting progressed it became clear that it was in effect rigged to promote a party and partisan line. The undergraduates who dominated the discussion were October Club men whose line was adroit but determined. They were for peace and against war, but *not for every kind of peace* and *not against all war*. They were against "imperialist war" but not against class war. They wanted imperialist nations to remain at peace, but they definitely did not want peace and concord within the body politic. Argument ensued in which I took some part along with several elderly League of Nations liberals, but the October boys were fiery and were in the ascendant numerically. The Chairman, Dr. David Ross, became more and more baffled and then irritated, but to no avail. I had the impression that he was thoroughly confused as well as definitely annoyed. Altogether it was a strange meeting, but I should probably have thought little of it and have forgotten the whole episode had not a curious encounter taken place a few days later.

I happened to be in Balliol College one evening in the rooms of a friend when a man came in who was introduced to me as the President of the October Club. I recognized him instantly as an American, of Jewish background and a graduate of Princeton University, whom I had met casually two years earlier at a Seminar on the Philosophy of St. Thomas Aquinas offered at Campion Hall, Oxford, by the brilliant Jesuit, Father Martin C. D'Arcy. I said: "———, didn't I know you at Father D'Arcy's Seminar two years ago?" He replied, his hands moving like flails and with ardent fervor: "Why yes, that's so and I remember you. Then I had before me the question, Catholicism or Communism: I was wavering between the two: but now there's no doubt. It's Communism." The words, the voice, the gestures, the quickly given witness, were those of a convert, a devotee, and a fanatic.

WHY COMMUNISM APPEALS

All that has happened subsequently vindicates this conception of Communism as a faith embodied in an orthodox dogmatic religion of an extreme authoritarian character. Such a view explains, incidentally, the strong appeal of

Communism, especially in the 1930's, to so many intellectuals, college and university undergraduates, young men and women of well-to-do, prominent, and even wealthy families. The Christian religion was on the defensive—it had been on the defensive in our universities for a long time. Yet youth was hungry and thirsty—as it always is—for a satisfying religion, for a meaningful and appealing interpretation of life and the world. Communism moved into the vacuum of spirit thus created. Its claim to be not religion but science undoubtedly facilitated its success in making converts from the intellectual classes.

This is the answer to the question which people ask constantly after lectures or in discussions on the Communist issue: "How could a man like Alger Hiss (or some one else) be a Communist"? We are in the presence of a phenomenon that is essentially religious in its psychology. Communism in our era presents some of the most extraordinary examples of faith, conversion, and sacrifice in the entire history of religion. It has also augmented to an unbelievable degree the dark debit side of religion—the ancient, oft-repeated, appalling tale of man's fanaticism, hypocrisy, inhumanity, and spiritual barbarism. In fact the motto of Communism might well be the psychologically shrewd epigram: "He who believes nothing can be made to believe anything."

An Exuberant Materialism

What is the Communist conception of the Supreme Real? What takes the place of God or Spirit or the All? The answer involves one of the strangest paradoxes in the history of religion, of philosophy, and of man. The Ultimate, declaimed Marx and his followers ever since, is the realization that there is no God and that Matter is All. Marx without doubt felt a fierce joy in being able to confess atheism. He felt in some way that he had found release and liberation. Never before was there a materialist so exuberant and optimistic.

The reason is clear. Marx's atheism was really phony. What had been effected in his soul and mind was a transference to a new, active, and purposeful—if a hidden and extremely mysterious—deity. His Matter, on examination, proves to have a most peculiar way of behaving. It behaves in a regular and quite predictable manner—exactly the way that a misguided spiritualist or idealist philosopher Hegel held up as the dialectical path traveled by Spirit in its creation and development of nature, man, and history. There is, therefore, meaning to the world. History is not a vast tissue of irregular and uncoordinated accidents. It has an end. It is going somewhere. It is possible for man to know scientifically this end, which is perfect Communism *via* bloody revolution and temporary dictatorship, and, if he wills to do so, to climb on the band-wagon of history. To do so is to affirm life; to reject the new Gospel is to perish in the embrace of an order that is dying.

Here we have a faith, a missionary enterprise, a call to conversion. We have also, as in every example of a virile faith, an implicit worship which moulds character and conduct. The mould is contributed by the god worshipped. In this case the deity is matter working by inexorable predetermination. The outcome ethically, politically, and socially was predictable and has infallibly come to pass, to the horror and consternation of mankind.

All laws and moral sanctions safeguarding the dignity and rights of the individual in society were thrown out as so much rubbish. Human life became cheap to a degree unknown since the Pharaohs. The only thing that counted was advancing, within the Dictatorship, the cause of rationalizing thoroughly an entire society, and laboring, in the outside world, in the strictest obedience to party-orders and without ever reasoning why, to promote the ultimate goal of world revolution, world dictatorship, and (mockery of faith! yet how powerful is man's will to believe!) world Communism—a universal classless Utopia.

This strains our credulity. It is impossible to believe men could be so evil. So the world of good men, notably the great sector of opinion in the United States and in Great Britain that is Protestant in religion and liberal in sentiment, continues in a haze of confused indecisiveness with respect to the real nature of Communism and with respect to the fact of War—war that is upon us—a religious war on the most colossal scale in history—a war in a world made one by science for the soul as well as the body of the human race.

Divorce of Reason and Love

The explanation of this phenomenon—so astounding because so unexpected—is not so difficult as we make it. It lies in an absolute divorce between reason and love. When this separation took place, under the sponsorship, on the one hand, of atheistic materialism, and, on the other, of faith in the supremacy of dialectic, establishing, as it were, scientific control on a faked supernatural and superhuman level, the way was opened for an eruption of evil forces on a scale and with an intensity that are without parallel. It is as if "the Beast that is chained in the abyss" had been let loose for a season to do his worst under the most favorable conditions. For there is nothing so demonic as reason entirely divorced from the moral will. It becomes in such case a pure instrument—a naked means of achieving the ends projected by unregenerate and unchecked imagination.

Such divorce is not absolutely novel. But the modern position of reason as a result of science and its child technology is novel and unique. It is this instrument, augmented and swollen to overpowering proportions by the discoveries and techniques of the twentieth century, which in the all-powerful police state has been freed from every restraint and moral inhibition. It is generally recognized in the free world that this happened in Germany under Hitler. What we are strangely slow to see is that Hitler derived his main inspiration from Russian Communism and that there was always the closest affinity between the two tyrannies. The German affair, terrible as it was, proved to be a flash in the pan (a) because Hitler was in too great a hurry, (b) because he and his henchmen lacked the long discipline in rational dialectics that Marxists have always insisted on, and (c) because the German people were too moralized and Christianized by long habit and tradition to be as amenable to total rationalization and regimentation as the Russians, eight-five per cent of whom were serfs at the time of the Bolshevik revolution.

The point, however, on which we must focus at the moment is the relationship between basic conception of the Real and results in ethics, politics, society, human values and goals. Perhaps never before have we seen an example of this relationship as clear and unconfused as that spread before us in the contemporary religion of Communism.

CHRISTIAN VIEW OF REALITY

What of Christianity? There is strong evidence, as we have seen in the last chapter, that it will not be superseded by any other religion or, as some people today hope and even predict, by a new revelation. A powerful affinity, rooted in history, exists between Christianity and democracy. The same, despite not a little disruptive tension, is true of Christianity and science. It is in every way likely that the religion of Christ, reinvigorated and rekindled by the assaults made upon it and the criticisms, not always unjustly, levelled at it in the modernist era, will win out in the death-struggle already forced upon it by a violent and confident adversary, the religion of Communism. What, therefore, does Christianity have to offer? What is the Christian interpretation of Reality?

The answer involves the clearest and most direct joining of issues both with atheism and with all forms of pantheism. Christianity sees the world not as self-existent and independent but as created and sustained by a living Will. Creation is the first term of the Christian view of the Real and is one of two keys to the uniqueness of Christianity among all systems constructed by men out of experience and faith.

Creation is pivotal and indispensable as a concept not because in itself it explains everything or clears away all difficult questions. On the contrary, it is an idea drawn from man's experience of making (the mechanical analogy) and creating (the artistic and dramatic analogy). It is a very helpful and useful illustration but it takes us only so far. The mystery of Divine Creation, involving the origination of the energy which is the basic "stuff" or "matter" of the universe, remains. This is a commendation of the doctrine of Creation, and not a criticism, for on every view of the Ultimate there remains the infinite and unexplainable. Man is finite, and it is not given to him "to pluck out the heart of the mystery." If any man claims the contrary, from pulpit or laboratory or in the street, he thereby proclaims himself a charlatan and is to be shunned.

Creation does, however, have two notable advantages as an interpretation of the universe. It allows the world to be world, nature to be nature, matter to be matter, mind to be mind, freedom to be freedom, individuality to be individuality. Here it has a very real affinity with materialism and naturalism. The Old Testament, in comparison with the Hindu Scriptures or with the writings of idealistic philosophers from Plato down, is a very earthy and realistic document. It betrays no tendency to tidy up the world and hastily hide the not so attractive linens of human nature before they are spread out for general inspection. It assumes with an incomparable innocence the unity of body and soul, the physical and spiritual, in the human being. Christianity conserves, emphasizes, and hallows this realism and wholeness in its mighty symbol of "the resurrection of the body."

This points up the second great advantage of the doctrine of Creation. It does not simply leave one immersed in the factualness of the given world, and there you are. This, curiously, is the result of pantheistic views (everything is God) quite as much as it is of materialism and atheism. But in the case of the creationist interpretation you have as the prior term in the cosmic process an intelligent, purposeful, living Creator. This means that things are never just what they are, and that is that. Things are what they are, *plus God*. They come from God and go to God. There is purpose, there is meaning, there is a goal. There is One who is ultimate Security and eternal Peace.

DOCTRINE THAT GOD IS LOVE

If the first key-idea in the Christian interpretation of the Real is that of a living, creative Will, the second is that God is Love.

To many this statement will sound sentimental, perhaps banal. Ours is a hard-boiled, tough-minded, "brutalitarian" age. It is an era of fire and sword, destruction and slaughter, enslavement and torture. There are many, this being our undoubted common background, to whom such a view of the Ultimately Real is like a red rag arousing anger. To others it seems simply absurd—a preposterous phantasy. To still others it is just unreal. There is no vital connection between such a concept of God and their experience.

With all these reactions I deeply sympathize. For many years the love of God was to me the least meaningful of Christian doctrines. Though I was an ordained minister and an authorized and respected theologian, I dwelt as little as possible on this doctrine, which incidentally is the crown of New Testament thought and the starting point of a thinker like Augustine and a poet like Dante. On the righteousness of God and the reality of judgment, yes! On man's inherent sinfulness and his frail finitude and helplessness, yes! On the Divine holiness and unapproachable majesty—on the *mysterium tremendum* before which man like Abraham of old is "dust and ashes"—on "the infinite qualitative distinction between God and man," yes! But on the love of God, His goodness and mercy, His fatherly compassion and infinite forgiveness, no! I could not dwell on these with joy and a sense of personal rapport and meaningfulness. I felt that they were soft and sentimental thoughts, constituting a doctrine of Divine indulgence.

Today I have a very different point of view. I believe that St. John was right when he asserted: "God is love." I think that St. Augustine was in touch with Reality when he inverted the Apostle's statement and reiterated: "Love (*dilectio*) is God"; "Charity (*caritas*) is God." This being so, continued the Saint, "to act against love is to act against God." I am ready to confess with Dante that the desire and

will of man have in them a motion derived from the same
Love "that moves the sun in Heaven and all the stars." I hear
with Charles Wesley

> . . . thy whisper in my heart!
> The morning breaks, the shadows flee;
> Pure universal love thou art;
> To me, to all, thy mercies move;
> Thy nature and thy name is Love.

These confessions and assertions are misunderstood if they
are taken as ebullitions of pious sentimentality. They are not
lyric ecstasies unrelated to life and normal experience. They
are poetic perhaps—is it Pringle-Pattison who once declared
his willingness to believe that only so much philosophy as
has been made poetry is permanent?—but they are expressions of a clear, well considered faith. It is a faith, as every
final interpretation of Reality is. The chief reason for this
faith is Jesus Christ—a man in whom men for nearly twenty
centuries have seen the unconditioned God. "No one has
ever seen God; the only Son, who is in the bosom of the
Father, he has made him known."[1] "And the Word became
flesh and dwelt among us, full of grace and truth; we have
beheld his glory, glory as of the only Son from the Father."[2]
The Christian doctrine that the Supreme Real is love is
initially and always principally an inference from the life,
the words, the death, and the resurrection of Christ. The
career, the impact on history, the abiding, deathless influence
of this Figure is the greatest miracle of all time. If any one
thinks he can explain it on natural grounds, he is at liberty
to try. He will soon find, however, that he is like a man
hacking away at a stone mountain with a cold chisel.

A second reason for believing in the Christian interpreta-

[1] St. John 1:18, RSV.
[2] *Ibid.* 1:14, RSV.

tion of Reality is modern psychiatry and depth-psychology. In a new, strong light it is revealed that love is the essential nature of man. In love he is conceived, born, and nourished. By love he grows, develops, and thrives. It is love which he craves from the cradle to maturity, and from maturity to the grave. Even hate, expressed in many aggressions and mean cruelties, is misplaced or distorted or frustrated love. The destiny of man, it seems, positively or negatively, is love. He cannot escape his nature. We may say that Freud, in not a few ways a second Augustine, is one of the major modern prophets preparing the way for the coming in new splendor and power of Christ the Lord of love.

Thirdly, it is for every man, in the light of experience, with the full use of reason, to consider and weigh the final alternatives. What is the nature of the Ultimate and Supreme? Is it matter—godless, blind, and at the source impelled by a necessity indistinguishable from chance? Is it power—naked, arbitrary, and harsh—above reason, law, or love? (This is the typically Semitic image: it is far from absent in the Old Testament, it is classically expressed in Mohammedanism, it has reappeared at various times in the Christian West, it lurks as a black cloud over the police state and the totalitarian idea in the present phase of Communism.) Is it pure reason, either personified or conceived as an impersonal order making our world a cosmos (Aristotle, Spinoza, Einstein, Jeans)? Is it a blind unconscious force, striving to manifest itself in the urge of life and the upthrust of evolution (the early Bergson, Bernard Shaw, some emergent evolutionists)? Or is Christianity true in that doctrine which is its heart and soul: is the Ultimate a living Will whose nature is Love? Is the Supreme "our Father" in heaven, "from whom all fatherhood in heaven and on earth is named"?[3]

[3] Ephesians 3:15, RV, Margin.

In the end every man must make his own decision, aiding or hindering the true God whose Spirit pervades the whole world and reaches out to touch every rational being. But decide he must. The election and the worship of some god is the fate of every man alive.

PRACTICAL RESULTS OF CHRISTIANITY

But what about the results, practically, of the Christian interpretation of the Real? How have the doctrines of Creation and the Love of God worked out in terms of life, conduct, the relations of man to man, the ordering of society? One is tempted to give the answer of G. K. Chesterton, that it is untrue to say Christianity has failed; it has never been tried. This, however, would be an insincere fudge. It would also lead one to neglect the very important problem faced by every religion and world-view when it is put into practice, namely, that the transition from the ideal to the real, from the inspired individual to the life of the multitudes, inevitably involves a process of reduction, dilution, and popularization. The ability to accept and at the same time transcend *this law of embodiment* is the test of the vitality of any religious system. From this standpoint Christianity scores high among the religions of mankind, ancient and modern.

Returning to the query, What of Christianity in practice? it cannot be questioned that it changed the world. The new calendar, symbolizing Christ as the hinge of history and the beginner of a fresh dispensation, was appropriate in the light of coming events and, in all probability, will never be superseded. It is Emerson who has said that the name of Jesus is not so much written as ploughed into history. We have seen in an earlier chapter how drastically the outlook of man on himself and his world was changed as a result of Christ, and how profound and revolutionary the consequences of this change have been. Among these are clearly to be enumerated the dawn of the age of reason, the birth and progress of modern science, the rise of democracy, the industrial and technical revolutions still in full swing.

In the field of ethics and social morality the results of Christianity, indirect as well as direct, have been far-reaching. The key-principle in a long and complex development is the worth of the individual and the obligation of preserving human life. Outcomes of the penetration by this principle of civilized mentality are: the rejection of infanticide, the abolition of slavery, the equality of woman, monogamy in marriage, unprecedented developments in medicine, nursing, and hospitals, social services, the care of the aged, the incurable, and the mentally ill, and psychiatry, with its remarkable emphasis upon the individual, his problems, history, dignity, and worth.

This doubtless is but one side of the picture. Western civilization in the past two hundred years shows profound weakness as well as immense strength. To unravel the whole intricate pattern of cause and effect, in this matter, would be an impossible task. Even to say generally whether Christianity is principally the cause or the victim in the process of gathering deterioration, destined to come to a climax in the middle of the twentieth century, would be hazardous and highly debatable. Perhaps to do so would be like undertaking to decide the issue of the priority of chick or egg.

SECOND LAW OF HUMAN NATURE

What is certain is that man, though created in and for love, also resists this law of his being and sets up in opposition to it a second tendency—an innate self-centeredness. This second law is what the Christian Church has called in the past *original sin*. It is the universal source of division, frustration, and actual deeds of evil. It is not repealed as a law of human nature simply by being ignored or denied. Such denial took place at the high tide of the age of reason. It was implicit in the whole idea of the inherent reasonableness and perfectibility of man—perhaps the leading thought of the eighteenth century and one of the two leading ideas (along with evolution) of the nineteenth century.

The result clearly has not been the universal advancement of love and brotherhood. On the contrary, this rational individualism co-operating with the impersonal and mechanistic tendencies of industrialism has promoted a process of depersonalization and dehumanization that has been very powerful and very fatal during the past one hundred and fifty years. This process involves, unconsciously, losing sight of man as a child of God, whose nature is love, for he is created in the Divine image; and thinking of him instead as a thing —an impersonal factor in a vast mechanistic order.

It was at a certain point in this development that Karl Marx arose. Marxist Communism as a religion is related to Christianity and European civilization in the nineteenth century very much as Mohammendanism was to Judaism and the Semitic culture of Arabia in the first decades of the seventh century. What Marx did, so disastrously, was to embrace as real and ultimate the impersonal, materialistic, a-moral, and non-human. In ethics he threw out love in favor of force—unconditionally from the immediate standpoint. The modern totalitarian police state is the outcome of this drastic and demonic decision. To be sure, Marx was a human being. He could not escape the first law of man's being, which is love. (The same thing is true even of tyrants like Napoleon, Hitler, and Stalin.) Out of the depths of his Judaic-Christian being there had arisen a cry for justice, a protest against oppression, an affirmation of brotherhood. These found expression in the vehemence of his indictment of the capitalistic industrial system and in the projection of a flawless, beautifully human utopia beyond the period of bloody violence to which it was his life-work to summon all workers and "true" intellectuals. These impulses were, in the main certainly, unconscious, for there was no integration of them with the ethics or fundamental philosophy of his system, and far from questioning the cold-blooded assumptions of *laissez-faire* economics, he adopted them without moral or philosophical criticism and devoted himself to deducing quite opposed social and political consequences.

ANTICHRIST

In any case, the tragedy of Communism and of our tortured contemporary world is that the denial of love as the first law of man's being has become a fixed dogma around which the most titanic and herculean efforts are being made to reintegrate the whole of human life and culture. It is this denial which is Antichrist, and which must be resisted by all possible means (save surrender to the Enemy's own principles) and with all the energy and resolution which free men and lovers of their kind can muster. This brings us, in conclusion, to a comparative summary of the two great opposing faiths—both of them religions of the West now in export to the East, reversing an ancient trend during many centuries—Communism and Christianity.

Communism is just over a hundred years old. In this short time it has made an amazing record. Beginning, as the poet Heine once remarked, in the garrets of Europe, it controls today the destiny of not less than eight hundred million of the earth's inhabitants. It is an immediate threat to several hundred million more. Such an achievement is bound to rest on something substantial. We live in a world of real cause and effect—not in a fairyland where things just happen. What is it that the Communists have?

Power of a Dream

The first thing that they have is a dream. There is an idea behind the dream; in fact there is a whole battery of ideas and theories, some of them very abstruse and not nearly so profound as they sound. But it is the dream—which is complete equality amid perfect plenty; it is the picture— which is a new, transformed, uncompetitive, warless and classless social order—that has captured the minds of men and given to a queer band of visionaries unheard of power.

The Communist dream has attracted men and women because it claims to be truth—this of course is the case with every powerful religion or philosophy. But the new faith has had *a special and characteristic attraction because of its complete this-worldliness*. Its dream is connected with the present world. It speaks of present social forces and scientific possibilities. It promises deliverance from present ills and evils. It offers bread, life, freedom, meaning here and now. It is in fact the first universal salvation religion to put its entire emphasis upon this life and this world. It is the first great secular religion—that is, the first on a world scale and with a completeness in content and development paralleling the great living faiths of mankind to be based on a denial of the transcendent and eternal.

This is the significance of Communism for all modern men and women. It did not just happen. The way for it was prepared by the advance guards of thorough-going rationalism —by secular liberalism, scientific humanism, and practical materialism. The psychological precondition for Communism, as for other totalitarian systems, was the creation of a spiritual vacuum in the soul of Western man through the loss of faith and through exclusive concentration on the things of this world. (Secular means, literally, referring to the present age or time or world.) From this standpoint Communism is not simply a mammoth evil let loose on mankind by an eternal devil. It is a symptom of disease and disorder in the body of Christian and liberal culture. It is the signal and flag, in disturbing red, of the advent of a new age and time. It is a spiritual challenge to every responsible human being. It is a summons to look to our own house and to look to it well.

A Naked Realism

The second thing that Communism has and that explains its astounding rise, is a naked and ruthless realism. This trait has its origin in the rejection by Marx himself of all idealism in favor of unqualified materialism and atheism. This led him to reject Christian ethics as well as theology and to posit his doctrines of the universal primacy of the class struggle and the absolute necessity of violent revolution and forceful dictatorship.

From this standpoint there is a very real continuity in Communism from Marx to Stalin and the police state that is the staple of existence for every people behind the iron curtain. Lenin wrote, at the time of the Russian revolution: "The basic question in any revolution is that of state power." This sentence has been the axiom of Communist strategy from its first bid for power. It will undoubtedly remain a primary axiom not only for revolutionary action but also for control and consolidation within every conquered society.

This is a very ominous and terrifying aspect of our present world. State power is potentially an absolute power. The State, as Hobbes said, is "that Leviathan", "a second god." In addition, there is a new factor in the ability of leaders today to communicate with the masses of the people easily and quickly. Never before was the manipulation of the multitudes possible in the way it is today. Never before was it possible to employ propaganda, indoctrination, education, discipline, and intimidation on the scale that is easily possible today because of modern communications, weapons, and transportation.

Practical realism based on utter ruthlessness and cynical dismissal of all normal "illusions" and sentiments, has been made a virtual science within the Communist Party. As the structure of the Party is rigidly hierarchical, this means that the science in question is evolved at the top and handed down. There is now available a careful study, not of the theories and ideas of Marxism-Leninism-Stalinism, but of the actual rules which are taught within the Party as requisite for political effectiveness. This study is by Nathan Leites and is embodied in a volume entitled *The Operational Code of the Politburo*. It presents what might be called the "moral theology" of Communism. A wag might be tempted to label it "the immoral theology." Actually these terms do not exist for Communist theory. The only thing that exists from this standpoint is that which advances or that which hinders the cause of Communism in the world.

CODE OF POLITBURO

A few examples may be given from a rich mine of material. They bring home, with something of the force of a bath in ice-water, the character of our adversary.

The only permissible question about any policy under consideration by the Party is: Will it enhance the power of the Party?

When the Party carries out a correct line, it "does not invent" anything . . . The party "solves the problem that has been put on the agenda by history."

The Party must not fall into despair if certain gains take much longer than had been estimated. On a historical scale, such differences in rate of development are minor.

Party policy must not be influenced by feelings or moral consideration . . . A "real" Bolshevik Party finds it easy to conduct an expedient policy, which from a "sentimental" point of view would be extremely repulsive (e.g. breaking a strike) . . . "A Communist who says that one should never dirty one's hands . . . that he is going to build a Communist society with clean . . . hands, is an empty phrasemaker."

"Replacing objective analysis by 'feelings' "—to *any* extent—threatens catastrophe.

A Bolshevik must have perfect control over his feelings. All his political activity is "a most coldblooded . . . war."

A Bolshevik must not feel insulted by any kind of behavior that outsiders may show toward him . . . must not act out of feelings of offense.

The Party must arrive at every one of its policy decisions on the basis of an intensive and repeated process of calculation. "We must act according to the rule, 'measure your cloth seven times before you cut.' "

This paradoxical combination of the dream in a materialized form and of cynical realism almost idealized, is something new in the history of religion and of man. It is a combination that is extremely powerful. It appeals to various sides of human nature at divergent levels of development and susceptibility. It is well suited to the mentality of our period—a mentality that has been subjected to many stresses and strains, that is disillusioned and yet believes, that feels the necessity of brutal tough-mindedness and yet is unable to throw off the spell of Utopian hope. It may well be that from this standpoint Communism has more quick assets than Christianity. From the standpoint, however, of a longer look and of resources for persistence and creative adaptive development, the advantage is all with Christianity.

RADICAL WEAKNESS OF COMMUNISM

Communism is too simple. Its basic materialistic analysis, while containing much truth and while important as a corrective alike to thought and to life, is an abstraction from the total facts of the world. The result distorts and caricatures Reality. It puts man into a straitjacket which is unbearable and which it is inconceivable he will endure for long. Indeed the ultimate judgment upon Communism is its self-contradiction and self-condemnation. It originated as a protest—somewhat concealed underneath the armor-plate of its intellectual and scientific pretensions, but genuine and prophetic—against the giant inhuman mechanism of the new industrial order, with its tendency to treat man as a commodity and thing to be bought and sold in the market to the highest bidder. It has ended, in less than a century, by being more radically inhuman than the order against which it originally protested. It reduces man not merely to an animal level; it regards and treats him as a thing, one material force and factor among an illimitable number. It makes him a pure robot, without rights, dignity, or legal protection, to be conditioned according to plan, used in relation to need, and rejected or liquidated as expediency may dictate. It puts him lower than serfdom, into a slavery more pitiless than any the civilized West at least has ever known. Communism in fact is not so much revolution as reversion; it is reaction and regression behind the great Liberal Revolutions, Feudalism, and Caesarism to the slavery and total tyranny of the great early empires. It is Neo-Pharaoism.

These are strong words. Some will disbelieve them. Others will feel they are too unqualified. Certainly there is no pride of prophecy or claim of special revelation in them. If they should prove unjustified, and signs of real democracy and humanity should appear where now total regimentation and brutal ruthlessness are all that one can discern, I would be happy and thankful. Unfortunately the facts are quite otherwise and all previous experience points in the contrary direction. A particular feature of Communism as a system is the total absence in it of any element of self-correction. There is only one party, and it is rigidly hierarchical and autocratic. There are no constitutional checks and balances. There are no independent courts. There is no tolerance of free inquiry, critical judgment, or objective, unslanted research. Science is as much a department of the totality, all rigidly under one control in thought, word, and deed, as the police, education, or the stage. Even the Church, which in Hitler's Germany in both its Catholic and Evangelical divisions gave so magnificent an account of itself, writing new chapters in mankind's golden book of heroes, saints, and martyrs, appears to be a "safe" section of the whole, determined to deserve its uneasy toleration by being as Stalinist as it was once Tsarist.

All, in short, is under the Party, and it is one mind, one will, even one heart in aim, moving from the apex of the pyramid down. All holes are plugged. The coldest and most ruthless realism in history has, with the ready aid of modern techniques, communications, and weapons, done an airtight job. It has sealed in the peoples of Russia and confederate or conquered states, as in a tomb. Its leaders and high priests, the men of the Kremlin, are imprisoned in the same tomb. Their freedom is even less. They are bound by the twin chains of the corruption of absolute power and the pitiless logic of an unexamined and sacrosanct dogmatism. They are compelled to exclude not only light and air, but also "mercy, pity, peace, and love."

ASSETS OF CHRISTIANITY

Christianity against such a background makes a strong appeal. It shines with a new beauty. Its historic failures, the feeble practice of so many of its adherents, its weariness and lack of novelty and "time-appeal," seem relatively minor. Its supreme asset, the Figure of Christ, the man who came not as a warrior, not as a philosopher, not as a Judge, but as a Friend and Lover, as the Affirmer absolutely of the glory of sacrifice and the reality of forgiveness,—takes on a new meaning and shines in the darkness of the world with a new glow and beauty.

Christianity cannot promise as much immediately as Communism. It cannot and will not compromise with the technique of "the Big Lie." Its founder, who claimed to be the Truth, did not offer men an easy entrance into the Kingdom of God. He seems to have noted with a certain exultation that He brought into life not placidness and ease, but storm and vitality. "From the days of John the Baptist until now the kingdom of heaven has suffered violence, and men of violence take it by force [that is, crowd in and push up, like soldiers storming a fortress]."[4] As He himself approached death, He warned the over-eager, ambitious sons of Thunder, James and John:

The cup that I drink you will drink; and with the baptism with which I am baptized, you will be baptized; but to sit at my right hand or at my left is not mine to grant; but it is for those for whom it has been prepared.[5]

Such words are sobering. They draw us up sharply and make us think. In the end, however, they are exhilarating and fascinating. Their attraction is much greater than that of an easy moral and social soporific. They certainly need not dampen true ardor, genuine enthusiasm, real hope. For the religion of Christ, which must always be viewed not onesidedly but as a whole, does have that which is able to heal, to inspire, and to save the world.

It has a God who is above and greater than man, or the state, or society, or the whole created universe. We say of this God that He is transcendent and eternal. This means that He is not to be identified ever with man or history or nature. This truth emerges in our day as truly vital and relevant, for we see once again how prone man is to idolatry and self-deification. It is as if modern history were arranged to illustrate the thesis of the eminent psychologist, Jung, that one of man's basic drives is "godalmightiness." This aboveness of God is for Christianity always and everywhere a principle of humility and self-correction.

Then Christianity has a view of man that is supreme in its balancing of affirmation with realism. It asserts the creation of man in the image of God, whose very being is Love. This means that the primary principle and law of the being of

---

[4] St. Matthew 11:12, RSV.
[5] St. Mark 10:39, 40, RSV.

man is love and goodness. But Christianity has always discerned and affirmed a division in human nature. Man has in him a deep contradiction. There dwells in him from birth and infancy a second principle or law—an omnipresent self-centeredness. In consequence, he has a strong bias toward extreme selfishness and this constantly thwarts and confuses the good and benevolent impulses of his social, appetitive, and rational being. The grand result is the whole array of passions, lusts, conflicts, complexes, neuroses, and worse, that afflict and complicate the life of the individual personality and that are writ large in a still more involved and exaggerated form in the collective evils of mankind.

This fundamental analysis is of the most notable practical importance. It yields what we may call *the Christian principle of provisional imperfection*. The Christian, if he knows what he is about, is like God in being very patient, very tolerant, and very forgiving. He knows that there is redemption, which means redirection of will from self to God and other lives; and he sees the reality of this in Christ, in the Saints, in mature Christians, and, it may be, in other elect souls. The Church exists to be the agent, even more, the very organ and body of Christ, in carrying through to life the power of redeeming love. But the Christian knows that this is a long, slow, and ever to be repeated process. He knows the futility and unreality of expecting perfection on easy terms. He is, therefore, prepared for evil and trouble, and has resources for dealing with them. He is cheered by what G. K. Chesterton's priest called "the good news of original sin." He is still more cheered and empowered by the knowledge of the love and forgiveness shown us not in abstraction but in our existence by Jesus Christ. He knows that here is medicine for all ills and an answer, if we have the courage and the faith to try it in earnest, to the Communist attempt to cement with brutality and blood a new society.

CHRISTIANITY AND A BETTER WORLD

This brings us to a final principle of Christianity, which we may call a temperate and realistic optimism. Here we have in mind the social aspirations of our period and the impatient longing of mankind in general for a better world. We have in mind by comparison "the dream" of Communism.

Christianity occupies, we believe, a position of commanding promise in relation to the vexed issue of materialism and idealism, exclusive this-worldliness *versus* escapist other-worldliness. The late Archbishop William Temple is the author of a famous saying—which is, however, by way of being misquoted very nearly as often as Lord Acton's memorable sentence on the corrupting effect of absolute power. What Temple wrote was: "Christianity . . . is the most avowedly materialist of all the great religions."[6] He goes on to express the view that Christianity because it recognizes the real existence of matter and gives it due credit, may hope to show the way to controlling it.

To some extent this is a new insight. The Lord's Prayer, it is true, includes prominent reference to "our daily bread." The Bible in both Testaments puts great weight on the created, the earthly, the bodily. Hebrew psychology was very physiological. The Christian Church has always placed in a very central position both particular sacraments and the sacramental idea as a key to the understanding of the universe and the ways of God. In its theology and its poetry it has spoken of "the resurrection of the body" and of a new,

[6] *Nature, Man and God* (New York: The Macmillan Co.), p. 478.

transformed heaven and earth. Its "kingdom of heaven" is an earthly and political image. In spite, however, of these materialist affiliations Christianity has tended through most of its history to be deflected toward Platonist and mystical other-worldliness. It has tended to emphasize the eternal at the expense of the temporal. Marxism was, from one angle, a savage protest against this whole tradition. Today most theologians would put greater weight, with Temple, on the wholeness of life and the impossibility of abstracting the spiritual from the organic and physical.

This is in no way to emulate Marxism by surrendering to the obviously unreal and false idea that matter is all. Here there are strong safeguards in the teaching of Christ, though they have sometimes been over-stressed. "Man does not live by bread alone," was one of His replies to the Tempter. "My kingdom is not of this world," He is reported to have answered to Pontius Pilate. He put strong emphasis on simplicity, moderation, and at times on poverty and asceticism. He had no illusions as to man's ability or fruitfulness apart from God. Being rich toward God, based on poverty of spirit or humility expressing itself in faith, He held up as the one essential.

Here we move in territory that has never been completely charted and that is full of quicksands and morasses. When, however, all the *pros* and *cons* are weighed, we assert confidently that Christianity has the best balance theoretically and practically in relation to the problem of matter and spirit which it is possible to attain, and has unique resources for meeting the aspirations of our urgent, material-minded, scientific, democratic age without falling into the slough of nihilistic materialism.

We close, very concretely, as the Book of Revelation closes, as the rival system of Marxist Communism concludes, by asserting what is to come. The picture which we present is not a Utopia. It is rather a vision of what our world as it is now, with all its problems and the drags inherent in it, yet with the magnificent resources, spiritual and material, which God has given His children, might reasonably become. This superb picture, a Christian dream for our society and world, was drawn by one already referred to, possibly the greatest Christian personality of our time, William Temple. May every reader return again and again to be inspired by his vision:

... We seem to see a vast multitude drawn from all races and from every social class pledged to one thing and to one thing only, the acknowledgment of God's sovereignty by obedience to His purpose in every department of life. As they labour there takes shape a world, much like our own and yet how different! Still city and country life with all their manifold pursuits and interests, but no leading into captivity and no complaining in our streets; still richer and poorer, but no thoughtless luxury, no grinding destitution; still sorrow, but no bitterness; still failure, but no oppression; still priest and people, yet both alike unitedly presenting before the eternal Father the one true sacrifice of dedicated life—the Body broken and the Blood outpoured; still Church and World, yet both together celebrating unintermittently that divine service which is the service of mankind.[7]

[7] William Temple, *The Hope of a New World* (London: Student Christian Movement Press, 1940), pages 124-125.

EPILOGUE

Three Remarkable Prophecies[1]

1. HEINE ON GERMANY, COMMUNISM, AND RUSSIA

Christianity has—and that is its fairest merit—somewhat mitigated that brutal German lust for battle. But it could not destroy it; and once the taming talisman, the Cross, is broken, the savagery of the old battlers will flare up again, the insane rage of which Nordic bards have so much to say and sing. That talisman is brittle. The day will come when it will pitiably collapse. Then the old stone gods will rise from forgotten rubble and rub the dust of a thousand years from their eyes; and Thor will leap up and with his giant hammer start smashing Gothic cathedrals . . . and when you hear a crash as nothing ever crashed in world history, you will know that the German thunder has hit the mark. At that sound the eagles will fall dead from the sky and the lions in the farthest desert of Africa will pull in their tails and slink away into their royal caves. A play will be performed that will make the French Revolution seem like a harmless idyll in comparison.

—*Religion and Philosophy in Germany* (1834); see
Works, Ed., Leland (London, 1892), Vol. V

Communism is the name of the terrible antagonist which sets agrarian rule in all its consequences in opposition to the *bourgeois regime* of to-day. It will be a terrible conflict—how will it end? *That* the gods and goddesses only know who know the future. This much do we know, that Communism, though it be at present but little discussed, and now yearns away its life in forgotten garrets on wretched straw-pallets, is still the gloomy hero to whom a great if transitory part is assigned in the modern tragedy, and which only

[1] See also the prophecy of the theologian Maurice quoted *supra,* p. 139. Maurice was a contemporary of Heine and De Tocqueville. Apparently the period around 1840 was a prescient and psychic time.

waits its cue (*Stichwort, replique*) to enter on the stage. . . . The second (act) will be European or the world Revolution, the gigantic battle of the disinherited with the inheritors of fortune, and in that there will be no question of nationality or of religion, for there will be but one fatherland, the Earth, and but one religion, that of happiness in *this* life. Will the religious doctrines of the past in every country unite to a desperate resistance, and thus form a third act in the great play? Or will the old Absolute tradition enter again on the stage, but this time in new costume and with new watchwords to incite and goad? How will this drama end? I do not know, but I think that at last the head of the great water-snake will be crushed, and the skin pulled over the head of the bear of the North. And then perhaps there will be only *one* flock and *one* shepherd—a free shepherd with an iron crook—and one great herd of men all shorn and all bleating alike. Wild and gloomy times come roaring on, and the prophet who would write a new Apocalypse must imagine new beasts, and those so terrible that the old symbols of St. John as compared to them will seem like soft doves and amorets. The gods hide their faces out of pity to the sons of mankind, their nurslings for so many years, and perhaps out of fear as to their own fate. The future has an odour as of Russian leather, blood, blasphemy, and much beating with the knout. I advise our descendants to come into the world with thick skins.

—Written in 1842; see *Works*, Vol. VIII

2. De Tocqueville on Russia and the United States

The time will therefore come when one hundred and fifty millions of men will be living in North America, equal in condition, the progeny of one race, owing their origin to the same cause, and preserving the same civilization, the same language, the same religion, the same habits, the same manners, and imbued with the same opinions, propagated under the same forms. The rest is uncertain, but this is certain; and it is a fact new to the world—a fact fraught with such portentous consequences as to baffle the efforts even of the imagination.

· There are, at the present time, two great nations in the world which seem to tend toward the same end, although they started from different points: I allude to the Russians and the Americans. Both of them have grown up unnoticed; and while the attention of mankind was directed elsewhere, they have suddenly assumed a most prominent place among the nations; and the world learned their existence and their greatness at almost the same time.

All other nations seem to have nearly reached their natural limits, and only to be charged with the maintenance of their power; but these are still in the act of growth; all the others are stopped, or continue to advance with extreme difficulty; these are proceeding with ease and with celerity along a path to which the human eye can assign no term. The American struggles against the natural obstacles which oppose him; the adversaries of the Russian are men; the former combats the wilderness and savage life; the latter, civilization with all its weapons and its arts: the conquests of the one are therefore gained by the plowshare; those of the other by the sword. The Anglo-American relies upon personal interest to accomplish his ends, and gives free scope to the unguided exertions and common sense of the citizens; the Russian centers all the authority of society in a single arm: the principal instrument of the former is freedom; the latter servitude. Their starting point is different, and their courses are not the same; yet each of them seems to be marked out by the will of Heaven to sway the destinies of half the globe.

—*Democracy in America* (1835)

3. Henry Adams on Russia and China

My statesmanship is still all in China, where the last struggle for power is to come. China is bound to go to pieces, and every year is a long step to the bad. The only country now on the spot is Russia, and if Russia organizes China as an economical power the little drama of history will end in the overthrow of our clumsy Western civilization. We never can compete with Asia. . . . In that event I allow until 1950 to run our race out.[2]

[2] From a Letter written by Adams on March 22, 1903, included in his published Letters, and recently quoted in the press. It was called to my attention by Mrs. John A. Church.

A Select Bibliography

For the Reader who desires to go further.

BENNETT, JOHN COLEMAN: *Christianity and Communism*, New York, Associated Press, 1948.

"BARNABAS": *Christian Witness in Communist China*, New York, Morehouse-Gorham Co., 1951.

BARRON, J. B., and WADDAMS, H. M.: *Communism and the Churches*, New York, Morehouse-Gorham Co., 1950.

BURNS, CECIL DELISLE: *Handbook of Marxism*, London, Victor Gollancz, Ltd.

CROSSMAN, RICHARD, Ed.: *The God That Failed* (Six studies by Ex-Communists), New York, Harper & Bros., 1949.

HALLOWELL, JOHN H.: *Main Currents in Modern Political Thought*, New York, Henry Holt & Co., 1950.

HEIMANN, EDUARD: *Communism, Fascism or Democracy?*, New York, W. W. Norton & Co., 1938.

———: *Freedom and Order,* New York, Chas. Scribner's Sons, 1947.

KOESTLER, ARTHUR: *Darkness at Noon*, New York, Modern Library, 1946.

———: *The Yogi and the Commissar*, New York, The Macmillan Co.

LEITES, NATHAN: *The Operational Code of the Politburo*, New York, McGraw-Hill Book Company, 1951.

LENIN, V. I.: *Selected Works*, 2 vols., Moscow, Foreign Languages Publishing House, 1946.

MARX, KARL: *Capital, The Communist Manifesto, and Other Writings*, Edited by Max Eastman. New York, The Modern Library, 1932.

MAURIAC, DUCATTILLON, and OTHERS (including BERDYAEV and DE ROUGEMONT), translated from the French by S. F. Scanlan: *Communism and Christians*, Westminster, Md., The Newman Press, 1949.

OAKESHOTT, MICHAEL: *The Social and Political Doctrines of Contemporary Europe,* Cambridge, University Press, 1939.

SHEED, FRANCIS J.: *Communism and Man*, New York, Sheed and Ward, 1938.

SHEEN, FULTON JOHN: *Communism and the Conscience of the West,* Indianapolis, Bobbs-Merrill Co., 1948.

SPERBER, MANES: *The Burned Bramble* (A novel of the Communist movement between the wars in Europe), Garden City, Doubleday & Co., 1951.

TEMPLE, WILLIAM: *Christianity and Social Order*, London, Penguin Special, 1942.

WALSH, EDMUND ALOYSIUS: *Total Empire; the Roots and Progress of World Communism*, Milwaukee, Bruce Publishing Co., 1951.

WHALE, J. S.: *Christian Doctrine*, New York, The Macmillan Co., 1948.